THE
EVERYTHING®
TODDLER ACTIVITIES
BOOK
2ND EDITION

Dear Reader,

Your toddler is at an exciting stage of their development. He is growing rapidly and gaining many new skills. You have an amazing opportunity to promote your child's emotional, social, physical and cognitive development all while still having fun!

You don't need to break the bank to occupy, educate and entertain your toddler. Put away the expensive toy catalogs and craft kits. Your toddler will respond to simple games and activities that keep her involved.

Your toddler is bound to keep you on the go. You will be able to use many of the ides in this book with no materials and no advanced planning. I hope that you will turn to this book again and again for ideas and inspiration!

Welcome to the EVERYTHING® Series!

These handy, accessible books give you all you need to tackle a difficult project, gain a new hobby, comprehend a fascinating topic, prepare for an exam, or even brush up on something you learned back in school but have since forgotten.

You can choose to read an Everything® book from cover to cover or just pick out the information you want from our four useful boxes: e-questions, e-facts, e-alerts, and e-ssentials.

We give you everything you need to know on the subject, but throw in a lot of fun stuff along the way, too.

We now have more than 400 Everything® books in print, spanning such wide-ranging categories as weddings, pregnancy, cooking, music instruction, foreign language, crafts, pets, New Age, and so much more. When you're done reading them all, you can finally say you know Everything®!

QUESTION
Answers to common questions

FACT
Important snippets of information

ALERT
Urgent warnings

ESSENTIAL
Quick handy tips

PUBLISHER Karen Cooper

DIRECTOR OF ACQUISITIONS AND INNOVATION Paula Munier

MANAGING EDITOR, EVERYTHING® SERIES Lisa Laing

COPY CHIEF Casey Ebert

ASSISTANT PRODUCTION EDITOR Melanie Cordova

ACQUISITIONS EDITOR Brett Palana-Shanahan

SENIOR DEVELOPMENT EDITOR Brett Palana-Shanahan

EDITORIAL ASSISTANT Ross Weisman

EVERYTHING® SERIES COVER DESIGNER Erin Alexander

LAYOUT DESIGNERS Erin Dawson, Michelle Roy Kelly, Elisabeth Lariviere, Denise Wallace

Visit the entire Everything® series at *www.everything.com*

THE
EVERYTHING®
TODDLER
ACTIVITIES BOOK
2ND EDITION

Over 400 games and projects to
entertain and educate

Joni Levine, MEd

Avon, Massachusetts

For Lizzie, the daughter I used to only
dream about. You bring me more
joy than I ever imagined.

An Everything® Series Book.
Everything® and everything.com® are registered trademarks of F+W Media, Inc.

Published by Adams Media, a division of F+W Media, Inc.
57 Littlefield Street, Avon, MA 02322 U.S.A.
www.adamsmedia.com

ISBN 10: 1-4405-2978-7
ISBN 13: 978-1-4405-2978-8
eISBN 10: 1-4405-3049-1
eISBN 13: 978-1-4405-3049-4

Printed in the United States of America.

10 9 8 7 6

Library of Congress Cataloging-in-Publication Data
is available from the publisher.

This publication is designed to provide accurate and authoritative information with regard to the subject matter covered. It is sold with the understanding that the publisher is not engaged in rendering legal, accounting, or other professional advice. If legal advice or other expert assistance is required, the services of a competent professional person should be sought.

—From a *Declaration of Principles* jointly adopted by a Committee of the American Bar Association and a Committee of Publishers and Associations

Many of the designations used by manufacturers and sellers to distinguish their products are claimed as trademarks. Where those designations appear in this book and Adams Media was aware of a trademark claim, the designations have been printed with initial capital letters.

This book is available at quantity discounts for bulk purchases.
For information, please call 1-800-289-0963.

Contents

Acknowledgments

I have many people to thank for their help in support. Susan Holmes, for many ideas and lots of feedback. Ideas also came from Cathy Abraham, Terri Menzies, and Susan D. Smith. Robin Herbol provided artistic insight and a lot of support. I also wish to thank Barb Doyen, both agent and friend.

Top 10 Materials to Have on Hand for Toddler Activities

1. **Crayons:** Remove the labels from crayons when possible. For the younger child, fatter crayons work best.

2. **Construction paper:** Construction paper is very versatile. Be sure to keep a wide variety of colors on hand.

3. **Poster board:** Use poster board when you need a stronger, more durable paper.

4. **White craft glue:** You can also use rubber cement or school paste for most projects. Choose what works best for you and your child.

5. **Old magazines:** Old magazines are a wonderful source for collage and activity pictures. Nature and home-living magazines are the best for this.

6. **Scissors:** In addition to adult scissors for you, purchase a pair of safety scissors for your child. If you wish, you can also find beginners' guiding scissors and fancy-edged scissors at school supply stores.

7. **Felt-tip markers:** Markers are useful for adding small details to projects. Some manufacturers even make washable markers.

8. **Food coloring:** This is handy for coloring homemade dough and various other craft materials. Please note: It does stain.

9. **Recycled household materials:** You can reuse materials such as egg cartons, yarn scraps, toilet paper tubes, and boxes for many activities.

10. **Nontoxic tempera paint:** Tempera paint is an easy paint for your child to work with. It has a nice smooth texture and comes in many colors.

Introduction

AS THE PARENT OF a young child, you have a unique role and opportunity. You can add fun, learning, and enrichment to your child's life every day by spending some time and engaging your child in simple activities. Studies show that early home life and experiences have the strongest impact on a child's development and future success. There are many reasons why you may have picked up this book.

Perhaps you are looking for activities that will develop and strengthen the bond between you and your child. You know that one-on-one quality time is critical for your relationship, as well as for your child's social and emotional growth. Many of the activities in this book are nurturing activities. You will find also activities that will enhance communication and interaction between you and your child.

You may be looking for ways to make your own life easier. If you are juggling many responsibilities and roles each day, raising and caring for a toddler can be an additional challenge. Sometimes you simply need a way to occupy or entertain your young child for a few minutes. After all, most parents do not have the luxury of devoting all of their time to their child. There are telephone calls to make, dishes to wash, bills to pay, and more. In this book, you will find many quick and simple ideas, many of which require little advance planning and few (if any) materials. Furthermore, most of the activities in this book do not require that you set aside large chunks of time or go to specialty stores to track down materials. You will also find a special section in this book to help out when you need something on the spot to help your child calm down.

Perhaps you wish to do more activities with your child that will help him learn and develop. You want activities that will have a clear benefit for your child, such as promoting growth or helping with school-readiness skills. This is still the book for you! Young children learn best through playful, hands-on activities. Just about any activity in this book will benefit your child's growth and development. You will find activities that develop pre-literacy skills, motor development and coordination, social skills, concept development, mathematical skills, and more! It does not matter where your child is developmentally, you will find ideas to meet her needs.

This book is designed to make it easy for you to find just the right activity for your child. Each activity includes a suggested age group and a time estimate. You will even find activities designed especially with special needs children in mind. Activities are easy to follow with a clear list of materials needed and step-by-step directions.

Activities that may pose any safety concern include a warning and/or suggestions for keeping your child safe. Some activities do use small items or potential choking hazards, such as Styrofoam and balloons. All activities in this book should be done under the direct and constant supervision of an adult. Carefully use your best judgment in selecting safe activities for your child.

CHAPTER 1

All about Toddlers

The very first step in choosing activities for your toddler is to make sure that you understand her. You need to be familiar with what toddlers can and cannot do, what they enjoy, and what may frustrate them. You probably know better than to purchase a chemistry kit for your two-year-old or to ask your three-year-old to join you in a game of gin rummy. However, you may not know what toys are best to promote problem-solving skills or why sharing can be so difficult for a toddler.

What Are Toddlers Like?

Toddlerhood, which encompasses the ages of eighteen months to three years, is an exciting period of your child's development. You have most likely noticed that she's growing rapidly and quickly acquiring many new skills and abilities. It may seem to you that just yesterday she was an infant, very passive and dependent on you. Now you can see that she is on the threshold of becoming a full-fledged individual.

Your toddler is truly caught in a time of transition. She is just starting to develop her own sense of self. At first, her only knowledge of her identity was that she was united with you. During the first few months of her life, she developed an attachment to you (and you with her). Her first relationship was with you. Now, however, she is slowly starting to see herself as a separate person, and soon she will develop new relationships.

ESSENTIAL

This time of becoming an individual includes separation and can be difficult. However, it will be easier if your toddler feels securely attached to you. When she knows that she can rely on you for love, comfort, and reassurance, she will be emboldened to take those first tentative steps away from you.

Emotional Volatility

As your toddler develops, she acquires many new skills. Along with physical and cognitive development, she also is maturing emotionally. You may find that your toddler's emotions are very close to the surface. Like flipping a light switch, she may go from happy and calm to fussy and agitated. At this age, she is likely to be easily overwhelmed and frustrated. Your calm, patient demeanor will be beneficial as you help her cope with and appropriately express her emotions.

Desire for Independence

You have probably noticed your toddler beginning to show a desire for independence. No longer completely dependent on you, she may even resist you during care-giving routines. She may start to insist, "Me do it," or "Let me try." Your child is developing autonomy. It is important that you give her opportunities to have some independence and to be sure to recognize both her efforts and her accomplishments.

Desire for Power

Along with this new desire for independence comes the wish for some degree of control and power. Your toddler is starting to learn that she can influence both the events and the people around her. Feeling a sense of autonomy and power is an important emotional milestone. Children who are restricted in this area can become doubtful of their abilities and may be reluctant to try things or act independently later on.

In an effort to assert this desire for autonomy and control, some toddlers may become defiant. They start to challenge limits and say "No!" to your requests. If you recognize that these behaviors are not made out of spite, you will be better able to manage them with patience and humor.

Limitations

Keep in mind that although your toddler is acquiring many new skills, she still has many limitations. She is quite egocentric, meaning that she has difficulty understanding the world from the perspective of other people. This makes sharing and empathetic behavior a challenge.

Your toddler also has a long way to go in developing language skills. The second and third years of life are the times of the most rapid language growth. Some of the activities in this book take into account that some toddlers are still nonverbal, and will actually help to promote your child's language development.

How a Toddler Learns

Young children are naturally inquisitive. It may seem to you that your toddler is compelled to explore and touch everything he can. His horizons are broadening daily, and there is much for him to discover. With so much that is still so very new, there will be no other time in his life that he will be this eager to learn. Capitalize on this enthusiasm, and nurture this inquisitiveness through both your attitude and the activities that you plan.

Sensorimotor Exploration

Young children learn best through direct sensory and movement experiences. If you wanted to teach your toddler about camels, you could try a few different teaching techniques. To your child, the information that a camel is a quadruped mammal that mainly resides in desert regions of Africa is meaningless. Nor is showing him a photo of a camel a very effective way to develop an understanding of what a camel is. Instead, you must engage your child in a quest to learn about camels. The best strategy would be to take him to the zoo, where he has the opportunity to see, hear, and touch an actual camel.

Flashcards were once a very popular way to teach young children. Sometimes you will still see television demonstrations of "baby geniuses" who, with the help of flashcards, can name the state capitals or identify photographs of past presidents. You should know that these children have been drilled with memorization exercises and do not have a true understanding of the facts they are reciting.

According to psychologist Jean Piaget, toddlers are in the sensorimotor stage of development. During this stage, a toddler learns best through direct, hands-on, concrete experiences. The capacity to learn through pictures, symbols, and abstractions does not develop until a child is six or seven years old. This is the reason that you will not find any worksheet activities in this book. Instead, each activity is geared to take advantage of the way toddlers learn best—by playing, by touching, and by having fun!

Other Ways to Learn

Your toddler learns in three main ways: through direct instruction, through imitation, and through sensorimotor exploration. Through demonstration and verbal directives, for instance, you can help your child learn basic skills, such as how to brush his teeth. You are a powerful role model for your child, and your actions speak louder than words. Other behaviors and skills, therefore, your child will learn by imitating you. The most effective mode of learning, however, is through trial and error in sensorimotor exploration. Lessons that are relevant and that engage your child as an active participant will have the greatest impact.

How Activities Help Your Child

You will not find any traditional academic rote-learning exercises in this book. But don't worry—neither you nor your child will miss them. Just about every activity described here is aimed to help your child develop in at least one critical area, and all of them are simply fun!

Play is the work of young children. Through play activities, your child is exploring and discovering. Play is the most effective and powerful way for young children to learn. Some scientists have found evidence that play can sculpt the brain and build denser webs of neural connections. When children play, they literally exercise their brain cells and make them expand and grow—a physical development that happens as your child learns. Play activities engage your child and help her develop many skills, including vocabulary, problem solving, reading preparation, math comprehension, social skills, and more!

QUESTION

Are all play activities of equal value?
No. Although structured recreational activities and games do have value, the best activities are open-ended. Allow time for your child to choose and create her own play scenarios. She will benefit the most when she has the opportunity to explore the themes and ideas that are most important and relevant to her.

There are many different types of play activities, and each type addresses certain skills and promotes development. Here are just a few examples:

- **Cooking:** Develops math skills (counting and measuring), nutrition, and science concepts (prediction, cause and effect).

- **Art:** Develops creativity, emotional expression, symbolic representation, fine motor skills, large motor skills, cooperation, and spatial concepts.
- **Pretend play:** Develops social skills (cooperation, turn-taking, and sharing), language and vocabulary development, imagination, and emotional expression.
- **Puzzles:** Develops problem-solving skills, abstract reasoning, shape recognition, and spatial concepts.
- **Block building:** Develops a foundation for more advanced science comprehension including gravity, stability, weight, and balance.

Choosing Appropriate Activities

Not every activity designed for toddlers will be right for your child. This is true for the activities in this book as well. You may find activities that are appropriate now and then come back later, as your child develops, to find other activities that are worthwhile. How do you choose appropriate activities for your child?

Start with your child's interests and follow his lead. If he seems to enjoy spending time watching ants on the back porch, you may want to consider planning some activities about insect lore. If your child is afraid of clowns, you would avoid going to the circus. You can also let your child's interest dictate how long an activity lasts and when to repeat it.

ESSENTIAL

You want to choose activities that are a good match for your child's skills and abilities. Each activity in this book includes a recommended age range meant to serve as a general guideline. Some of the activities in this book are meant to engage young toddlers (beginning at eighteen months of age). Many other ideas presented here will be enjoyable for children as old as four and five.

Use your personal knowledge of your child's unique abilities to determine if an activity is appropriate. If an activity is too complex, he may become frustrated. On the other hand, activities that are too simple may bore him.

Although you want to choose activities that reflect your child's skill level, you don't have to worry about always keeping things easy. On occasion, go ahead and try an activity that poses some sort of challenge for your child. This doesn't mean something so difficult that he becomes confused or frustrated. Just keep an eye out for activities that allow your child to try something new, with your encouragement and guidance.

General Guidelines

There are ways for you to ensure that an activity is a fun and valuable experience for your toddler. Whether you are trying the activities in this book or those from another source, the following sections provide guidelines to help you.

Keep It Short

Most toddlers have a very short attention span. Do not expect your toddler to be any different. He is too young to focus on an activity for any length of time and is apt to be easily sidetracked—especially from quiet activities or those that require him to remain passive, such as storytelling. Most activities presented here can be done in less than twenty or thirty minutes. If you want to plan a solid half-hour of activity time for your child, it is a good idea to set up two or three short activities rather than one longer one.

Be flexible, and respond to your child. If you notice that he is losing interest in an activity, try to modify it to recapture his interest or simply move on to something else.

Guide Your Child

Toddlers like to feel competent, and that means they want to do things for themselves. This does not mean that you should set up an activity for your toddler and walk away. You need to be available to encourage and guide your child through all stages of each activity.

Although you do not want to "do" the activity for your child, it is acceptable to intervene if your child is having difficulty or showing signs of frustration. Gently make suggestions or ask questions to guide your child along. For example, if your child is having a hard time with a puzzle, you might say,

"Why not try the blue piece?" or "What other piece could you try?" With your guidance, your child will be able to master many new skills.

Reduce Waiting

Waiting is especially difficult for the young child who does not clearly grasp time concepts. You cannot expect your toddler to be patient for long. Avoid activities that call for children to be eliminated. A game like musical chairs is an example. Once the child is out, he is left, often frustrated and angry, to entertain himself.

Involve Your Child

The most valuable and fun activities are those that actively involve your toddler. Avoid activities that require your child to be passive—to just sit back and watch. You can adapt most activities to enhance your child's involvement depending on his interest and skill level. For example, when an activity requires cutting out pictures, you can let your older toddler help you. Keep your eyes open for opportunities to involve your child more. You might let him stir the batter in a cooking activity or help set up the boundaries for a game.

Keep Activities Open-Ended

Whenever possible, look for activities that encourage your child to make choices. For example, the main goal of art experiences for young children is to promote creativity and emotional expression. There is very little value in having your child follow a rigid pattern to create something that looks just like the thing you or anyone else could make.

In the world of childhood art, boats may look like bananas, cats may have three eyes, and the sky can be orange. In the world of childhood games, someone may be "it" twice in a row, and it is okay to pin the tail on the donkey's head. When rigid rules and restrictions are lifted, the real fun begins!

CHAPTER 2

Activities Throughout the Day

There may be times when you have the leisure to plan activities in advance for your toddler. However, there will certainly be many other times when you need to come up with something fun to occupy your toddler on the spot. The activities in this chapter are designed to fit into your normal daily routine without much effort or planning. You will find ways to entertain and involve your young child and to make any ordinary day more pleasurable for both you and your toddler.

Morning-Time Activities

Start your day on the right foot! These activities can help with routines and promote bonding with your toddler. Follow your child's lead; if they are not a "morning person" they will not enjoy too much stimulation early in the day.

Down by the Banks

Add some pizzazz and excitement the next time you bounce your little one on your knee.

ACTIVITY FOR AN INDIVIDUAL CHILD

Age group: 18–40 months

Duration of activity: 5 minutes

Chant the following words and use the corresponding actions:

Down by the banks of the Wanky Swanky
(bounce child on knees)
Where the bullfrogs jump from bank to banky
(lift child from one to knee to the other)
With a hip, hop, and hippity hop
(bounce child on knees)
They jump off the lily pad and land kerplop!
(lower child between your knees)

Matching Sock Game

Here is a fun way to promote classification skills. Don't be afraid to include your socks in this game.

ACTIVITY FOR AN INDIVIDUAL CHILD

Age group: 18–40 months

Duration of activity: 10 minutes

Socks of different colors and patterns

1. Place a pile of loose socks on the floor in front of your child.

2. Encourage your child to sort the socks by color or pattern.

Wake Up Tickles

Adjust the intensity of your touch to suit your child.
Some children find tickling to be an unpleasant sensation.

ACTIVITY FOR AN INDIVIDUAL CHILD

Age group: 12–40 months

Duration of activity: 5 minutes

Slowly wake your child by gently tickling parts of his body. Start with extremities such as fingers and toes and work toward his belly.

Tiptoe

Young children will enjoy the overexaggerated sense of suspense.

ACTIVITY FOR AN INDIVIDUAL CHILD

Age group: 18–40 months
Duration of activity: 5 minutes

1. Encourage your children to creep or tiptoe throughout the house as they get ready for the day.

2. You may wish to whisper and add to the excitement by pretending not to wake a sleeping giant or family member.

Bath-Time Activities

Bath time can be very soothing and calm. But there's also a dark side to getting clean—bath time can also be stressful, marked by battles and tantrums. It is not uncommon for children to resist the need to take a bath. Young toddlers often worry that they can slip down the drain. You can help make this a better experience with a very simple first step and just ensure that the water is a comfortable temperature. You will also find it helpful if you avoid rushing this routine and take the time to make things fun with these activities. To ensure the safety of your toddler at bath time, make sure that you eliminate all distractions. Turn on the answering machine, do not answer the door, and be sure to have all of your supplies close at hand.

Fizzy Bath Balls

Liven up your child's bath time with these homemade fizzy bath balls.
Your toddler can also participate in making them!

Makes 4–6 balls

Age group: 18–40 months

Duration of activity: 10 minutes to make and 1–2 days to dry

1 cup baking soda
½ cup citric acid
½ cup cornstarch
2 tablespoons coconut or almond oil
1 tablespoon water

1. Combine dry ingredients.

2. Mix oil and water, and drizzle onto dry ingredients while stirring. Stir to combine thoroughly.

3. Shape into balls. Allow to dry for 24–48 hours.

4. Add a fizzy ball to the bath water. The ball will fizz for a few minutes.

Soap Crayons

This activity combines an opportunity for creative expression with bathtub fun.
Your child can use these crayons to draw on the tile or on herself!

Makes 12 crayons

Age group: 18–40 months

Duration of activity: 15 minutes to make and 2 days to set

1 cup soap flakes or powder
3 tablespoons water
Washable tempera paint
Ice cube trays or small paper cups (for molds)

1. Mix soap and water together to make a stiff dough that can hold its own shape. Add more soap powder or water as needed to reach the desired consistency.

2. Divide the mixture into 3 or 4 balls. Add a few drops of paint to each portion to create desired colors.

3. Press mixture into molds and let set for a few days before using as crayons in the tub.

Bathtub Finger Paints

Most toddlers love to get messy. What better place for a messy activity than the bathtub?

ACTIVITY FOR AN INDIVIDUAL CHILD

Age group: 18–40 months
Duration of activity: 15 minutes

2 tablespoons liquid soap
1 tablespoon cornstarch
Food coloring

1. Mix all ingredients together for each color and store in covered containers. Mixture will last for a few weeks.

2. Let your child use the paints to paint on his body or on the tub tiles. When bath time is over, the paint will rinse away.

Fishing in the Tub

Children usually enjoy water play. Here is a way to make bath time a fun time.

ACTIVITY FOR AN INDIVIDUAL CHILD

Age group: 18–40 months
Duration of activity: 15 minutes

Toy plastic fish
1 small aquarium net

Simply add the toy fish to the bath water for your toddler to catch with the net. If you don't have toy fish, you can cut out some simple creatures from craft foam, or even a kitchen sponge!

Calming and Rest-Time Activities

Your toddler needs his rest. It is recommended that your toddler get twelve to fourteen hours of sleep in a twenty-four-hour period. It is often very difficult for young children to shift gears. They are unable to go from being active and wound-up to calm and restful without a transitional time. In other words, it is unrealistic to expect that your toddler will be able to go directly from chasing butterflies to a long and peaceful nap. Try to have a set routine with calming activities in place to assist your child in unwinding and preparing to rest.

Back Blackboard

Try this to help calm your child before bedtime.
You can also massage your child's hands and feet this way.

ACTIVITY FOR AN INDIVIDUAL CHILD

Age group: 18–40 months
Duration of activity: 10 minutes

Body lotion, if desired

1. Ask your child to lie still on his stomach. Direct him to pay attention to what he feels.

2. Use your finger to draw on your child's back. For younger children, make shapes and spirals. For the older child, you can draw specific shapes, letters, or numbers and ask him to guess what they are. Use lotion for a variation.

Roll Up

Tucking in your child at bedtime can be part of a soothing ritual.

ACTIVITY FOR AN INDIVIDUAL CHILD

Age group: 18–40 months
Duration of activity: 5 minutes

Bed
Extra blanket

1. Spread the blanket out on top of your child's made bed.

2. Have your child lie on top of the blanket on one side of the bed.

3. Tuck the near side of the blanket over him and gently roll him across the bed until he is wrapped up in the blanket roll. Unroll your child before you leave him to go to sleep.

Monster Spray

Help your child use his imagination to conquer his fears and get a good night's rest.

ACTIVITY FOR AN INDIVIDUAL CHILD

Age group: 18–40 months
Duration of activity: 10 minutes

1 empty spray bottle
Materials for decorating (markers, stickers, etc.)

1. Have your toddler decorate the bottle.

2. Tell the child that this is now a bottle of monster repellent. Let him spray wherever he thinks there could be monsters lurking!

Counting Sheep

Counting sheep is a well-known way to cure insomnia. Try this cute game to help lull your toddler to sleep. Supervision is needed if your child is still prone to putting things in his mouth.

ACTIVITY FOR AN INDIVIDUAL CHILD

Age group: 30–40 months

Duration of activity: 10 minutes

8 to 10 cotton balls

1. Tell your child that the cotton balls are little sheep. Show him how he can herd them all on the pillow one by one. Perhaps they can hide under the covers, too!

2. Be sure to remind him that sheep are timid and that if he gets up or makes noise, the sheep will be frightened. If you are ambitious, you can use craft pompoms and draw on eyes for more realistic sheep.

Mealtime and Cooking Activities

Mealtimes can be a great way to interact with your toddler and make her feel involved. When you include your child in mealtime activities and preparation, she is more likely to eat the food that you are serving. Additionally, cooking activities will help her learn about nutrition, as well as science and math concepts such as fractions, measurement, evaporation, and more.

Personal Placemats

Your child will enjoy creating her own placemat that she can use at every mealtime.
She may want to make one for each person in your family.

ACTIVITY FOR AN INDIVIDUAL CHILD

Age group: 18–40 months
Duration of activity: 15 minutes

12" x 14" sheet of poster board
Crayons or markers
Clear contact paper

1. Have your child decorate both sides of the poster board with crayons and markers.

2. Use clear contact paper to laminate her creation.

Homemade Butter

This activity is a lot easier than you would imagine.
While making butter, your child is developing large motor skills and observing scientific changes as well.

ACTIVITY FOR AN INDIVIDUAL CHILD

Age group: 18–40 months
Duration of activity: 20 minutes

1 cup heavy cream
1 clear jar with a lid
1 marble

1. Put the heavy cream in the jar with a marble. Cover jar with lid.

2. Have your child shake the jar vigorously until butter forms. Enjoy your fresh butter on some hot rolls!

Rainbow Toast

Your toddler will enjoy decorating her toast with many colors.
This is fun to make and fun to eat!

ACTIVITY FOR AN INDIVIDUAL CHILD OR A GROUP

Age group: 30–40 months
Duration of activity: 10 minutes

½ cup milk
Food coloring
Cotton swabs
2 slices white bread

1. Divide the milk into 4 or more portions in small containers. An empty Styrofoam egg carton works well.

2. Help your child place a few drops of food coloring in each milk portion to create the colors she desires.

3. Have child use the cotton swabs as paintbrushes to paint colorful milk designs on the bread. Be sure they don't get too soggy.

4. Toast the bread under a broiler.

Mini Pizzas

Pizza may very well be the most popular food among children.
Here is a way to involve your child in mealtimes and spark her creativity, too.

ACTIVITY FOR AN INDIVIDUAL CHILD OR A GROUP

Age group: 30–40 months
Duration of activity: 20 minutes

1 canned biscuit
1 tablespoon tomato sauce
1 teaspoon grated mozzarella cheese
Toppings as desired: pepperoni slices, onion rings, green pepper slices, etc.

1. Help your toddler pat the biscuit dough out into a circle, then help her spread on the sauce and cheese.

2. Let your child choose and arrange the toppings for her pizza. One idea is to use to pepperoni slices and a green pepper slice to make a smiley face.

3. Bake the pizza in a toaster oven or under the broiler until the cheese melts.

Transition Times

A typical day involves more than waking, eating, dressing, bathing, and playing. A chunk of the day is also taken up by transition times, going from one routine to another. These simple activities will help you keep your child on task and motivated. Cleanup and chore times will also go more smoothly with these ideas.

Bend and Stretch

Here is a cute way to get your toddler up and moving in the morning.

ACTIVITY FOR AN INDIVIDUAL CHILD

Age group: 18–40 months
Duration of activity: 5 minutes

Teach your child this simple rhyme and the motions that correspond with it.

Bend and stretch
Reach for the sky
Stand on tippy toes
Oh so high

Bend and stretch
Reach for the stars
Wave your arms
Both near and so far

Cleanup Is Fun!

Cleanup time does not have to be a battle. Simply make cleaning up a game!

ACTIVITY FOR AN INDIVIDUAL CHILD

Age group: 30–40 months
Duration of activity: 15 minutes

1. Explain to your child that all of his toys have homes, or special places where they belong. Then explain that he needs to make sure none of his toys get lost and must help each one find its home again. (It is helpful to have special places designated for your child's belongings. You may want to label shelves and cubbies with pictures to help your child match what belongs there.)

2. Guide your child by having him pick up items by category. For example, you might say, "Let's pick up all the red things first." Alternately, set a timer and have him try to speed-clean to beat the clock.

This Is the Way

Just about any activity or routine is more fun when you are singing.

ACTIVITY FOR AN INDIVIDUAL CHILD

Age group: 18–40 months
Duration of activity: 5 minutes

Make up different verses to the tune of "Pop! Goes the Weasel." Here's an example:

This is the way we put on our shoes
Put on our shoes, put on our shoes
This is the way we put on our shoes,
So early in the morning.

Other potential verses might involve how to wash our face, wait for the bus, climb into bed, and so on. You can change the time of day as appropriate—to "late in the evening," for example.

Helping Around the House

The toddler years are an in-between time in terms of development. Your child is no longer a baby, but she is not yet fully a big child, either. You will see your child's interest in, and possibly her insistence on, becoming a big girl. "Me do" or "Let me" may be a common request from her. You can give your toddler a chance to feel competent by enlisting her help with your activities. Toddlers love to imitate, and yours can learn new skills while bonding with you.

Sock Sort

Laundry time can be a fun time to interact with your young child while teaching her sorting and classification skills.

ACTIVITY FOR AN INDIVIDUAL CHILD

Age group: 30–40 months
Duration of activity: 15 minutes

Show your toddler how to sort socks. You can have her put socks in piles according to color, style, or size. See if your toddler is able to match up sock pairs.

Washing Fun

*Most toddlers enjoy water play, so they will truly love feeling
as if they are helping you with this fun activity.*

ACTIVITY FOR AN INDIVIDUAL CHILD

Age group: 18–40 months

Duration of activity: 15 minutes

1. The next time you are washing dishes or other items, set up a bin with some soapy water.

2. Give your toddler a sponge, and let her wash her toys. Alternatively, let your child join you in hosing off the patio or even washing the car!

Side by Side

*Give your toddler a chance to feel like a big kid. Your child's interest in imitation and interaction
with you is all the motivation she needs to help out with the chores.*

ACTIVITY FOR AN INDIVIDUAL CHILD

Age group: 18–40 months

Duration of activity: 20 minutes

Buy your child a little whisk broom to help with sweeping. She may be able to help push the vacuum cleaner, but many toddlers are frightened by the sound. Additionally, you can give your child a damp rag and let her help you with the dusting.

Anytime Activities

There may be many times throughout the day when you'll need or want to keep your toddler busy with an activity. Perhaps he has grown tired of his new toy, or maybe you just want him to stay off the kitchen floor that you just finished cleaning. Whether you have five minutes or an entire afternoon, the activities in this section will fill the bill.

Fill and Dump

You will be surprised to see how much young children like to fill and dump containers. An added plus is that this activity helps them learn about cause and effect.

ACTIVITY FOR AN INDIVIDUAL CHILD

Age group: 18–40 months

Duration of activity: 20 minutes

Small containers, such as Tupperware or coffee cans

Small toys, such as blocks, balls, or collectable toys. Be sure that the items do not pose a choking hazard.

1. Seat your toddler on a blanket or rug.

2. Give him the containers and the little toys. Demonstrate the game by putting a few items into a container and then dumping them out.

3. Give your toddler the containers and let him fill and dump them on his own.

Where Is My Pair?

*You can set this game up in a snap. Not only is it a lot of fun,
it will also help your child with problem-solving skills.*

ACTIVITY FOR AN INDIVIDUAL CHILD

Age group: 18–40 months

Duration of activity: 10 minutes

Pairs of items, such as socks, mittens, or
   shoes
A box or laundry basket

1. Divide all the pairs, placing one mate in the box and one in plain view somewhere else in the room.

2. Remove an item from the box. Show it to your toddler and ask him to find its mate and make a pair.

Water Paint

*This is a great outdoor activity. It is up to you to "sell" this activity, and once you do,
your toddler's imagination will take over and make this a lot of fun.*

ACTIVITY FOR AN INDIVIDUAL CHILD

Age group: 18–40 months

Duration of activity: 25 minutes

Small container of water
Paintbrushes

1. Take your child outside, or seat him in the bathtub.

2. Tell him that the water is imagination paint and he can paint whatever he wants.

3. As he paints, ask him to describe what colors and patterns he is making.

Treasure Hunt

This game is easy to set up and will entertain your toddler for quite a while.

ACTIVITY FOR AN INDIVIDUAL CHILD

Age group: 30–40 months

Duration of activity: 15 minutes

1 roll of crepe paper (a long ribbon may be substituted instead)

Favorite toy or prize

1. Thread the streamer in a trail around the room or house. Weave it around the couch, under the table, and so on—the goal is to make an interesting and challenging path for your child to follow.

2. Attach a favorite toy or a small prize at the end of the streamer for your child to find.

3. Give your child the loose end and have him follow along the path to find the treasure.

Window Clings

You and your child can make these decorations to suit any season or interest.

ACTIVITY FOR AN INDIVIDUAL CHILD

Age group: 30–40 months

Duration of activity: 25 minutes

Food coloring, various colors

White craft glue in small bottles

Sheet of clear flexible plastic, such as those used for transparencies

1. Mix food coloring with glue, a different color in each bottle.

2. Let your child squeeze the glue onto the transparency to create his picture or design. Filled areas work better than outlines. You can place a pattern under the clear sheet as a template for a design. Leave a hole at the top of your design for hanging the decoration later.

3. Let dry for 1 day and remove from plastic.

4. Thread a length of string or fishing line through the hole; hang decoration in front of a window.

5. To store, wrap securely in plastic wrap and keep in a cool place.

CHAPTER 3

What to Do on a Rainy Day

What do you do when the weather is rainy or cold, and your child is stuck inside all day? Dr. Seuss addressed this problem in one of his best-known stories, *The Cat in the Hat*. The children in this story seemed to be doomed to sit forlornly by the window watching the rain, until the Cat in the Hat comes to entertain. Fortunately you don't need to juggle fish or fly a kite in the kitchen to turn a gray day into a fun day.

Shake Out Your Sillies

Young children need plenty of opportunities to move around. They need time and space to run and romp. You can usually meet this need by allowing your child to go outside, but what do you do when the weather is bad? Here are some indoor activities that will give your child a chance to burn some of her pent-up energy.

Beanbag Toss

This is a classic activity that will help your child develop motor skills.
If you don't have beanbags, you can simply use rolled-up socks.

ACTIVITY FOR AN INDIVIDUAL CHILD OR A GROUP

Age group: 18–40 months
Duration of activity: 10 minutes

Several beanbags
An empty receptacle, such as a box or basket

1. Give your child 3 or 4 beanbags and show her how to gently toss them.

2. Be creative in choosing a receptacle. Empty boxes or laundry baskets work well.

3. Let your child toss the beanbags into the receptacle.

Shadow Dancing

Here is a great way to get your child moving. Perhaps you can get the whole family to join in.

ACTIVITY FOR AN INDIVIDUAL CHILD OR A GROUP

Age group: 18–40 months

Duration of activity: 15 minutes

A bright lamp
A light-colored wall
Favorite music recording

1. Position the lamp in the middle of the room, leaving plenty of space between the lamp and the wall.

2. Turn on the bright lamp and darken the rest of the room. Aim the lamp directly at the wall. Stand your toddler in front of the lamp so that her shadow is cast clearly on the wall.

3. Put on the music and encourage your child to dance so that her shadow dances, too. For a cool-down activity, show your child how to use her hand to create simple shadow puppets.

Indoor Obstacle Course

When your child is stuck indoors, you will be happy to have an activity that helps her use her large motor skills and burn off steam. You do want to stress to your child that this is a special activity that can only happen with your approval and supervision.

ACTIVITY FOR AN INDIVIDUAL CHILD

Age group: 30–40 months

Duration of activity: 30 minutes

Pillows
Blankets

1. Find a safe place in your home to set up a miniature obstacle course.

2. Set out pillows to use as stepping stones or hurdles. Use blankets to create tunnels. The path may also make your child navigate furniture, such as crawling under a table or climbing over the ottoman.

Toddler Twister

Here is a simplified version of the classic game that will help your child with color recognition. You can still use the commercial game mat or create your own playing space, as described below.

ACTIVITY FOR AN INDIVIDUAL CHILD

Age group: 30–40 months

Duration of activity: 15 minutes

Colored circles cut from construction paper (the size of a paper plate)

Masking tape

1. Tape the colored circles onto a hardwood or linoleum floor.

2. Call out one simple direction at a time—for example, "Put your foot on a blue spot." To add a challenge when your child has mastered the basic game, you can cut some of the circles into different shapes to test both her shape and color recognition.

When Bad Weather Threatens

When bad weather is approaching, you may be facing more of a challenge than entertaining your child. It is common for young children to be frightened of storms. You need to set a good example—if you remain calm and nonchalant, chances are your child will stay calm as well. These activities will keep your child occupied and may even distract him from his anxiety.

Storm Sounds

Be sensitive to your child's fears. If he doesn't like loud noises, he may not like this activity. However, some children who are frightened of thunder may feel a greater sense of control when they can safely duplicate the noise.

ACTIVITY FOR AN INDIVIDUAL CHILD

Age group: 18–40 months

Duration of activity: 30 minutes

Audio recording of thunder
Metal cookie sheets

1. Play the recording for your child. Discuss what he hears and try to figure out what is scary about the noises.

2. Show your child how to bang and rattle the metal cookie sheets to simulate the sound of thunder. Ask your child to come up with other ways to make thunder sounds, which may include banging on pots and pans or a toy drum.

Rain Sticks

Rain sticks have long been popular as musical instruments in other cultures. But you don't have to go to a fancy import store at the mall to buy one—your child can make one out of materials you have around the house. Many children find the sound of a rain stick to be very soothing.

ACTIVITY FOR AN INDIVIDUAL CHILD

Age group: 18–40 months

Duration of activity: 15 minutes

Crayons
1 cardboard paper towel tube
2 squares of tinfoil, large enough to cover the ends of the tube
Masking tape
1 long pipe cleaner twisted into a loose coil
¼ cup dry rice

1. Let your child color the tube for decoration.

2. Fasten 1 tinfoil square on the end of the tube with masking tape. Leave the other end open until the tube is filled.

3. Help your child fit the pipe cleaner into the tube. Assist her in pouring in the rice.

4. Close the other end of the tube with the second square of tinfoil. Show your child how to tilt the stick back and forth to create the rain noise.

Let's Go Out

You don't have to always stay in when the weather is dreary. You won't melt, and there is a lot of fun to be had during a warm summer's rain. Be sure to return inside if there is any lightening in the area.

Runny Pictures

Your child will enjoy livening up the yard with these beautiful but temporary creations.
This works well with chalk too.

ACTIVITY FOR AN INDIVIDUAL CHILD

Age group: 18–40 months
Duration of activity: 20 minutes

Water color paint
Paint brushes

1. Go outside before the rain comes or while it is just drizzling.

2. Let your child paint on the sidewalk or cement area to create any pictures he wishes.

3. Observe how the water makes the colors run.

Mini Streams

This is a great way to encourage your children to use observation and problem-solving skills.

ACTIVITY FOR AN INDIVIDUAL CHILD

Age group: 12–40 months
Duration of activity: 15 minutes

Sticks
A patch of dirt or sand outside

1. Show your child how to use a stick or his finger to create a small trench in a patch of dirt where the rainwater can flow.

2. Encourage him to clear leaves to create mini rivulets.

3. Show your child how to lead the paths so that the water flows downhill.

Storm Shelter

Once your shelter is built, you may wish to spend some cozy time in there snuggling or reading a story.

ACTIVITY FOR AN INDIVIDUAL CHILD

Age group: 24–40 months
Duration of activity: 30 minutes

Rain poncho or tarp
Clothes' pins or duct tape

1. Help your child spread a poncho or tarp to create a tent or lean-to. You may drape the cloth over a piece of patio furniture, a large branch, or a fence.

2. Use clothes' pins or duct tape to fasten as needed.

Collect Rain

Try this activity during different times when the rain fall is heavy and light.
Let your child explore further by transferring water from one container to another.

ACTIVITY FOR AN INDIVIDUAL CHILD

Age group: 12–40 months

Duration of activity: 15 minutes

Various sized containers

1. Involve your child in selecting different containers. Point out why some will work better: Wide necks, no holes etc.

2. Have your child experiment by placing the containers in different locations. Can she collect more rain if the container is under a drain spout or under a tree or out in the open?

A Day at the Beach—Indoors!

You don't have to wait until you win the lottery to spend a day in paradise. There is no better way to beat the winter blues than to have a day at the beach in your very own home. Don't be surprised if the rest of the family wants to join in on the fun.

Indoor Beach

With a little effort and creativity, it is easy to transform your living room into a wonderful surfside paradise. You can always find fun, tropical-themed props at your local party supply store, too.

ACTIVITY FOR AN INDIVIDUAL CHILD

Age group: 18–40 months

Duration of activity: 1 hour

Beach towels
Large umbrella
Scissors
Brown construction paper
Green crepe paper or ribbon
Wall adhesive (such as Sticky Tac)
Recording of beach-type music
Beach-theme posters (optional)

1. Set up the beach towels and the umbrella as you would if you were at the beach.

2. Cut out a palm tree trunk from the construction paper, and cut sections of crepe paper for the fronds. Crease each frond into a wide "V" before attaching them to the trunk. Post the completed palm tree on the wall using the wall adhesive.

3. Hang any other themed posters or props, and play your favorite tropical music.

Beachcomber

Here is a fun twist on a simple scavenger hunt. You can alter the complexity of the challenge based upon your child's ability.

ACTIVITY FOR AN INDIVIDUAL CHILD OR A GROUP

Age group: 18–40 months

Duration of activity: 15 minutes

Seashells (large enough so that they don't pose a choking hazard)
Small plastic pails, one for each child

1. Hide a number of seashells in a room. Make some easy to find, and choose more challenging hiding places for others.

2. Give each child a pail, and encourage all of them to find as many shells as they can.

Beach Fantasy

This activity will help your child develop motor skills as she exercises her imagination. You can add to the fun by having your child dress in appropriate beach attire, such as a swimsuit and sunglasses.

ACTIVITY FOR AN INDIVIDUAL CHILD OR A GROUP

Age group: 18–40 months

Duration of activity: 15 minutes

Ask your child to pantomime various actions that take place at a beach. Possibilities include swimming, jumping over the waves, walking on hot sand, or surfing.

Indoor Volleyball

This is a fun game for all ages. When you are playing with young children, take the emphasis off of completion and point scoring. If you are worried about using a ball inside, use a balloon instead. Watch for popped balloons as the pieces can be a choking hazard.

ACTIVITY FOR A GROUP

Age group: 30–40 months

Duration of activity: 20 minutes

Small beach ball
1 sheet or blanket

1. Hang the sheet between 2 chairs, low enough for players to see over the top while they are seated.

2. Divide children into 2 equal groups, and seat groups on opposite sides of the sheet.

3. Show players how to gently volley the ball or balloon over the sheet.

Fun with a Box

It is a common scenario: A young child excitedly tears through the fancy wrapping paper, ribbons, and bows. He opens the box and removes the year's newest and hottest technological gizmo toy. After a few minutes of play, he puts aside the toy and turns his attention and creativity to the toy he prefers—the box. In fact, boxes are wonderful open-ended toys. Rather than running on batteries, they run on imagination!

Treasure Chest

Young children tend to find and collect little treasures.
Many of these items may be meaningless and even bothersome to you, but they are dear to your child.
Make this project with your child and give him a special place to store his treasures.

ACTIVITY FOR AN INDIVIDUAL CHILD

Age group: 30–40 months

Duration of activity: 20 minutes

White craft glue

Wrapping paper or tissue paper cut to fit the outside of the box

Cardboard shoebox with a lid

Ribbons, buttons, fabric scraps, yarn, sequins, or any other crafty remnants available

Mailing label

Marker

1. Assist your child in gluing on the paper to cover the shoebox.

2. Provide him with many different materials to glue onto the box for decoration.

3. Apply the mailing label to the box and write your child's name on it. Find a special place to store the "treasure chest."

Box Train

There are many dramatic-play props that you can make with a box.
This project is just a suggestion to help spark your own ideas.
When cutting the rope, be sure that none of the sections are long enough to be a safety hazard.

ACTIVITY FOR AN INDIVIDUAL CHILD

Age group: 18–40 months

Duration of activity: 30 minutes

Three shoeboxes (or other small boxes open on top)

Scissors

Lightweight rope, cut into three 1' sections

Tempera paint or markers

Teddy bears, dolls, or action figures (to act as passengers)

1. Arrange boxes to form cars of the train. The front car is the engine—the open side of this box should be down, as the engine doesn't carry passengers. The other boxes are open side up.

2. Cut a small hole in the front and back sides of each box so that holes in all boxes line up.

3. Connect the boxes with the sections of rope. Knot the rope ends on the inside of each box to secure them. A rope in the front can be used to pull the train.

4. Let your child decorate the train with paint or markers. The train is then ready to carry its passengers.

Matching Boxes

Promote your toddler's problem-solving skills with this fun activity. You can do this at any time, but it's a particularly good way to use paper from a recent holiday or birthday.

ACTIVITY FOR AN INDIVIDUAL CHILD

Age group: 30–40 months

Duration of activity: 20 minutes

Wrapping paper in various patterns

Boxes with lids, in various sizes (shoeboxes and small gift boxes work well)

Scissors

Ribbons or bows (optional)

Transparent tape

1. Choose a different color or pattern of wrapping paper for each box and matching lid. Wrap separately so that you can remove the lids once the boxes are wrapped. If you wish, you can have your toddler help you decorate the boxes.

2. Place all of the boxes in one pile and put the lids in another pile. Have your child match up the boxes with the lids.

Nesting Boxes, Stacking Boxes

This activity will teach your toddler about size, spatial concepts, and problem solving while having fun. You may choose to have your child decorate the outside of the boxes.

ACTIVITY FOR AN INDIVIDUAL CHILD

Age group: 30–40 months

Duration of activity: 10 minutes

3–4 small boxes of diminishing size (without lids)

Challenge your child to nest the boxes inside of each other. Alternatively, ask him to try to stack them and build a tower.

Shoebox Golf

This game tests your young child's motor skills and eye-hand coordination.

ACTIVITY FOR AN INDIVIDUAL CHILD

Age group: 30–40 months

Duration of activity: 20 minutes

Scissors
1 shoebox
Crayons
Masking tape
1 golf or ping-pong ball

1. Cut a hole in the center of the shoebox lid just big enough to fit the golf ball.

2. Invite your child to decorate the inside of the lid with the crayons. (He can also decorate the rest of the box, but the inside of the lid is most visible as it is the playing field.)

3. Invert the lid and secure it over the empty box with a couple strips of masking tape. You want to be able to remove the lid to retrieve the ball.

4. Place the ball on the lid. Challenge your child to tilt the box back and forth and try to get the ball to fall in the hole.

Backward Upside-Down Day

The next time bad weather forces you to stay indoors with your child, why not make it into a special day? Try following the backward, upside-down theme throughout the day. Start the day by greeting your child with a "Good night!" Consider letting her wear some of her clothing backward. Maybe you can have breakfast as the last meal of the day. Here are some other ideas to get you started.

Backward Meal

Children of all ages will love the silliness of having a backward meal.
Don't be surprised when you are asked to do it again next week.

ACTIVITY FOR AN INDIVIDUAL CHILD OR A GROUP

Age group: 18–40 months
Duration of activity: 30 minutes

1. If your family has assigned seats at the table, consider a shift. Let your toddler sit at the head of the table for this meal.

2. Of course, a backward meal must start with dessert! You can go the extra step by serving the pie à la mode upside down.

3. For the main dish, how about a backward sandwich or tortilla wrap? Put the meat and cheese on the outside with the bread and dressing in between.

4. Let your child suggest other silly ideas. She might decide to wear her napkin on her head instead of in her lap or to use a fork for her pudding—why not?

Last-Minute Activities

As a parent, you know the saying about the best-laid plans. Sometimes you need to come up with a way to calm or entertain your child without much planning. Here are some ways to pull a little magic out of your hat.

Makeshift Shelters

Every child likes to create pretend places to play in.
This activity gets you involved in the fun—a great bonding experience.

ACTIVITY FOR AN INDIVIDUAL CHILD

Age group: 18–40 months

Duration of activity: 30 minutes or longer

"Building" materials, such as couch cushions, blankets, cardboard boxes, etc.

Help your child use the building materials to set up a fantasy environment where he can engage in pretend play for many hours. The shelter may become a tent, a fort, a cabin, a boat, a lighthouse, or a farm—the possibilities are endless.

Tea Party

This activity is fun for boys and girls. Instead of dolls, your child can invite favorite action figures or stuffed animals. This does not have to be an elaborate party. You can use real materials, but pretend props work just as well.

ACTIVITY FOR AN INDIVIDUAL CHILD

Age group: 30–40 months

Duration of activity: 20 minutes

1. Let your child help you plan and set up the event. What can you use for decorations? What will you serve?

2. Follow the level of your child's interest. You may simply need to put a few paper plates on a table, or your child may enjoy making placeholders, party hats, and so on.

3. Attend the party and be a good guest—enjoy the refreshments, and keep the conversation lively!

Rainy-Day Pictures

Do not despair the next time rainy weather keeps your child indoors. This fun rainy-day picture will help chase the blues away.

ACTIVITY FOR AN INDIVIDUAL CHILD

Age group: 30–40 months

Duration of activity: 20 minutes

Crayons
1 sheet white construction paper
3 or 4 large paper soufflé or baking cups
White craft glue
3 or 4 pieces of yarn, each 3" long

1. Let your child use the crayons to color a rainy-day picture.

2. Show your child how to make umbrellas. Fold the baking cups (which will double as umbrella tops) in half and glue to the rainy-day picture. Glue yarn "handles" to the picture underneath each umbrella top.

Indoor Snow Fun

Try these fun ideas when it is too cold to go out and play in the snow, or if you live in a warmer climate without snow. To add authenticity, give your child mittens and a scarf to dress up in while he is playing.

ACTIVITY FOR AN INDIVIDUAL CHILD

Age group: 18–40 months

Duration of activity: 45 minutes

White sheets
Cotton balls
White socks
Instant potato flakes

1. Drape the white sheets over furniture and on the floor to create a wintry look to the room.

2. With your child's help, toss around the cotton balls and pretend that they are giant snowflakes.

3. Wrap pairs of white socks into balls and use them for a pretend snowball fight.

4. Put the potato flakes in a pan for sensory pretend play. If real snow is available, bring some in and let your child play with it in a contained area.

Puzzle Hunt

Here's a new way to interest your child in puzzles and problem solving. It is best to use a puzzle that your child knows and can complete. Jumbo floor puzzles work best for this activity, but you can use any favorite jigsaw puzzle.

ACTIVITY FOR AN INDIVIDUAL CHILD

Age group: 30–40 months

Duration of activity: 15 minutes

1 puzzle with all the pieces

1. Remove 1 piece of the jigsaw puzzle and set it on a table. Hide the remaining puzzle pieces. You can choose how hard you want the search to be. For a younger child, you may wish to scatter the pieces in plain view and face up.

2. Bring your child into the room. Show him the single piece and explain that he needs to find the missing pieces in order to complete the puzzle.

CHAPTER 4

Away from Home

Although it may make your life easier, you cannot tote along all of your child's toys whenever you leave the house. Whether you are going on vacation or just a short trip to the post office, you can still engage your child in many fun and worthwhile activities. Most of these activities need no planning and few materials. You are sure to find some favorites here along with some new ideas that you can pull out of your hat when you need them.

Air-Travel Activities

Flying with young children can be a challenge. In such a confined space, restlessness and boredom will soon kick in for your naturally active toddler. Here are some simple ways to pass the time that will not disturb other passengers.

Name That Tune

This activity will help develop your toddler's listening skills while passing the time.

ACTIVITY FOR A GROUP

Age group: 30–40 months

Duration of activity: 20 minutes

1. One person softly hums a familiar tune, such as "Twinkle, Twinkle, Little Star."

2. The person who guesses gets the next turn at humming a tune.

Who Am I?

Here is a game that everyone can play. An added benefit is that it will promote your child's problem-solving skills. For older children, you can extend the categories to include people or even objects.

ACTIVITY FOR A GROUP

Age group: 18–40 months
Duration of activity: 20 minutes

1. One player thinks of an animal. The rest of the group asks yes-or-no questions—Do you fly? Are you small? Do you eat bugs?—to figure out what the person is thinking.

2. The person who guesses correctly takes the next turn at being an animal.

Touch Blue

This silly game is a more sedate version of Twister.
Young children will also be practicing color identification.

ACTIVITY FOR A GROUP

Age group: 18–40 months
Duration of activity: 15 minutes

1. One person takes the role of leader and calls out a different color for the players to touch.

2. The players must touch something nearby that is of the specified color. Players may touch objects that are within reach, including each other's clothing.

3. The next player takes a turn being the leader.

Car-Travel Activities

"Are we there yet?" This may be the mantra of young children traveling in the car. However, your next car trip can be a pleasant one if you have ways to occupy your children. Set aside a play kit for your child to be used only for car travel. Avoid small pieces that can be lost or become projectiles in an accident.

On the Road

Here is a fun way to prevent loose parts from flying all over your car.
When your child tires of roadway play, he can also use the tray with magnetized letters and toys.

ACTIVITY FOR AN INDIVIDUAL CHILD

Age group: 18–40 months

Duration of activity: 20 minutes

Adhesive magnet discs
Toy cars
Cookie sheet (or other metal tray that magnets will stick to)
Masking tape (optional)

1. Attach the magnets to the bottom of the toy cars.

2. Let your child drive the magnetized cars all around the tray.

3. If desired, help your child use masking tape to outline roadways on the tray.

Animal Sounds

This is a lively game to play the next time your family takes a drive through the countryside.

ACTIVITY FOR A GROUP

Age group: 18–40 months

Duration of activity: 30 minutes

1. Players look out for animals along the road.

2. When someone spots an animal, she identifies it by the sound it makes. For example, "I see a moo!"

In the Hospital

If your child is hospitalized or even bedridden at home, his activities will be limited. When he starts to feel better, staying in bed can be difficult. Here are some quiet activities that you can bring to him while he recuperates.

What Is Hiding?

This quiet activity can be played while your child is resting in bed.

ACTIVITY FOR AN INDIVIDUAL CHILD

Age group: 18–40 months

Duration of activity: 10 minutes

Familiar objects, such as a teddy bear, a book, an alarm clock, etc.
Blanket

1. Hide a familiar object, such as a teddy bear or alarm clock, under the blanket.

2. Ask your toddler to guess what is hiding under the blanket.

3. If he does not guess, slowly pull back the blanket to reveal more and more of the object until he guesses correctly.

Yarn Squiggles

Your toddler will be amazed at how the yarn will stick!
To create a new design, he can just remove the yarn and start over.

ACTIVITY FOR AN INDIVIDUAL CHILD

Age group: 18–40 months

Duration of activity: 20 minutes

White craft glue
1 large sheet sandpaper (big enough to cover poster board)
1 sheet heavy poster board or cardboard
A variety of yarn pieces in different colors and lengths

1. Glue the sandpaper onto the poster board to form a solid work surface.

2. Have your toddler arrange the yarn on the sandpaper. The yarn will stick on its own.

Easy Collage

Being stuck in bed does not mean that your child cannot enjoy a simple craft activity. Be mindful that small items may pose a choking hazard if your child still puts things in his mouth.

ACTIVITY FOR AN INDIVIDUAL CHILD

Age group: 18–40 months

Duration of activity: 20 minutes

Clear contact paper, twice the length of the poster board

1 piece of heavy poster board or cardboard

A variety of collage materials (felt, twigs, buttons, lace scraps, etc.)

1. Spread the contact paper flat on a table, sticky side up. Remove half of the protective paper.

2. Smooth the poster board over the sticky part of the contact paper. Fold the protected half over with the protective paper still on.

3. Let your child arrange the items on the poster board.

4. When he is satisfied, he can remove the paper from the top half of the contact paper and fix it on top of the design to keep the design pieces in place.

5. For variation, you can skip the poster board and create a sticky sandwich with the contact paper used as both the base and top of the project.

Paper Chain

You can sometimes find paper chain kits in the store, but it is cheaper and more fun to make your own.

ACTIVITY FOR AN INDIVIDUAL CHILD

Age group: 30–40 months

Duration of activity: 45 minutes

Scissors

Lightweight bond paper in various colors

Craft paste sticks

1. Cut out strips of paper 1" wide and 4" long. If your child is adept with safety scissors, he can help you.

2. Show your child how to apply a dab of paste with the paste stick and close each strip to make a link.

3. Help your child attach the links together.

4. When your child has completed a long chain, you hang it up to help brighten the room.

Activities to Do While Waiting

You can never have too many "anytime" activity ideas. There are many times when you need to find a way to occupy your child's attention. These activities are great fun whether you are waiting for a bus, sitting in a doctor's office, or you just want to take a few minutes to interact with your child. These are also great activities to share with other people who care for your child.

Favorites

Help pass the time by engaging your child in this simple game. As a bonus, this activity will help your child with categorization skills and will enhance her vocabulary development.

ACTIVITY FOR TWO OR MORE

Age group: 30–40 months

Duration of activity: 15 minutes

1. Take turns being the leader with your child. The leader names a category, like television shows, ice cream, or flowers.

2. Players take turns naming their favorite things within the category.

I Spy

This is the classic guessing game.
Your child will be using observational and problem-solving skills when she plays.

ACTIVITY FOR TWO OR MORE

Age group: 30–40 months
Duration of activity: 15 minutes

1. One person picks an object in the environment that is in plain view to all players. Then she recites the following chant, "I spy with my little eye something that is . . ." (red, tiny, fuzzy, and so on).

2. Other players try to guess what that person has spied. The first person to guess correctly then takes a turn "spying" something.

Here Comes Daddy!

This is a great game to play when you are waiting to meet someone,
like Daddy, in a public place. Depending on whom you plan to meet, this game might be called
"Here Comes Grandma!" or "Here Comes Mommy!"

ACTIVITY FOR TWO OR MORE

Age group: 30–40 months
Duration of activity: Variable

1. While waiting for Daddy, watch the other people who are walking past. Start the game by pointing out someone who is clearly not Daddy—the less like Daddy, the better. Enthusiastically, say "Here comes Daddy!"

2. The other person responds by pointing out someone who looks even less like Daddy and exclaiming, "No, here comes Daddy!"

3. Continue until Daddy arrives.

Handy Dandy

Here is a new version of a simple game.

ACTIVITY FOR AN INDIVIDUAL CHILD

Age group: 18–40 months

Duration of activity: 5 minutes

1 small object you can hide in your
   hands, such as a coin

1. Show the child both of your hands. Place a small object such as a coin or a piece of candy in one of your hands. Remember, don't let your child have the object if she is still putting things in her mouth.

2. Put your hands behind your back, and tell your child that you are moving the object from hand to hand.

3. Close your hands into fists and bring them back to the front of your body. Hold one hand higher than the other.

4. Recite the following poem and ask your child to guess which hand is holding the object:

    Handy dandy midley moe
    Which do you pick, the high or the low?

5. When your child picks the correct hand you can either give her the object to keep or let her take a turn at hiding it.

On the Spot—When Child Gets Fussy

Here are some quick and easy activities that you can do anytime and anywhere. Whenever you see that your child is starting to get fussy or you feel a tantrum could be around the corner, try one of these soothing ideas.

Cobbler Cobbler

Hold your child on your lap, or let him lie on his back so that you can play with his feet.

ACTIVITY FOR AN INDIVIDUAL CHILD

Age group: 12–40 months
Duration of activity: 5 minutes

Chant the following words and use the corresponding actions:

Cobbler, cobbler, mend my shoes
(wiggle his feet to and fro)
Have it done by half past two
Stitch it up and stitch it down
(tap lightly around the edges of his feet)
Now nail the heel all around
(hammer his heel gently with your fist)

Drumstick

This activity is built upon the classic toddler pastime of banging on pots;
your toddler may have already discovered this activity on his own.
Close supervision is needed, and you should be sure to talk about why this is only an outdoor activity.

ACTIVITY FOR AN INDIVIDUAL CHILD

Age group: 12–40 months
Duration of activity: 5 minutes

1. Give your child a drumstick to use as a tapper. You can make one by super-gluing a wooden bead onto a dowel rod. Or in a pinch, you can use a wooden spoon or even a popsicle stick.

2. Take your child outdoors and encourage him to tap on different things. Talk about what he hears. Possible items to tap include bricks, a tree trunk, and a rain gutter.

Real Finger Puppets

Add some pizzazz by taping some yarn or felt on for hair and clothing.

ACTIVITY FOR AN INDIVIDUAL CHILD

Age group: 12–40 months
Duration of activity: 15 minutes

Washable, nontoxic markers

1. Simply draw a face on each finger that you wish to use as a character. You may also wish to involve your child and use their fingers as well.

2. Create a simple play or act out a rhyme like "Little Miss Muffet."

Tape Pulling

Be sure to avoid industrial tape that will stick to the skin.

ACTIVITY FOR AN INDIVIDUAL CHILD

Age group: 12–18 months

Duration of activity: 5 minutes

Tape (any kind)

Give your child a strip of transparent or masking tape. Let him loop and stick and unstick the tape.

Beach Activities

It may not take much to entertain you when you spend a day at the beach. You may be content to lie in the sand, feeling the warm sun on your skin and listening to the sounds of the crashing waves. Your toddler, on the other hand, is not easily amused. Once she tires of digging in the sand, she may be ready to call it a day. Try some of these activities to make a day in the sun fun for everyone.

Beach Obstacle Course

All you need is a shovel and a stick to create a fun beach activity for your child.

ACTIVITY FOR AN INDIVIDUAL CHILD OR A GROUP

Age group: 18–40 months
Duration of activity: 15 minutes

A stick
Small plastic beach shovel

1. With the stick, draw a winding line in the sand to create a path for your child to follow.

2. Use the shovel to create ditches or gullies along the path for your child to jump over. You can also build up mounds for her to climb over or walk around.

Beach Towels

Here is a chance to let your child show her creativity and create something that she will enjoy using.

ACTIVITY FOR AN INDIVIDUAL CHILD

Age group: 18–40 months
Duration of activity: 15 minutes

Fabric paints in a variety of colors
Pie tins (one for each color)
Scissors
Sponges
Large light-colored towel

1. Empty each color of fabric paint into a separate pie tin.

2. Cut the sponges in beach-themed shapes (shells, starfish, fish, or suns).

3. Show your child how to dip the sponges into the paint and then press onto the towel to create a design.

4. Let the towel dry completely and follow the fabric paint manufacturer's instructions before using.

Beach Cast

This is a wonderful way for your child to preserve memories. Beach casts also make great gifts.

ACTIVITY FOR AN INDIVIDUAL CHILD

Age group: 18–40 months

Duration of activity: 15 minutes to prepare, 3 days to set

Small shovel

Wet sand

Pie tin or other small container

Seashells, driftwood, and other medium-sized beach items

Water

Plaster of Paris

1. Have your child shovel wet sand into the container to fill it about one third of the way.

2. Let her select items to add to the cast. Limit the items so that there is some space in between them.

3. Show your child how to press the items so they are securely stuck into the sand without being buried.

4. Mix water and plaster of Paris according to package directions.

5. Spoon the mixture over the sand and shells so that it reaches the rim of the container.

6. Let the cast dry for a few days then gently remove from the container and rinse off.

Zoo Activities

There is so much to explore at the zoo. Take your time; your child will enjoy his trip much more if you allow him to linger where he wishes. Many zoos now have interactive features for young children. Seek out the exhibits that offer hands-on learning opportunities.

Zoo Lotto

Enhance your child's interest and observational skills with this fun game.

1. Use the ruler and marker to outline six equal squares on the poster board.

2. Review the magazine pictures with your child. Let him select six pictures of animals that he thinks he will find at the zoo.

3. Help him glue one animal picture in each square.

4. Cover the board with clear contact paper.

5. Bring the board and dry-erase marker to the zoo. Show your child how to mark off each animal that he sees.

6. Challenge him to complete the entire card.

Move Like Me, Sound Like Me

Engage your child with this lively movement activity.

As you view an animal, ask your child to mimic how the animal moves and/or sounds. Good animals to imitate are monkeys, kangaroos, elephants, and the big cats.

Museum Activities

Not too long ago, taking children to a museum was an exercise in frustration, given all of the interesting things they could look at but not touch. Fortunately, children's museums in many larger cities now recognize that children learn best through hands-on exploration. Even some of the larger traditional museums have added more interactive exhibits. You can make any museum more interesting to your toddler with these simple ideas.

Can You See?

This is a version of the game I Spy.

ACTIVITY FOR AN INDIVIDUAL CHILD

Age group: 18–40 months

Duration of activity: 15 minutes

1. As you approach a picture or an exhibit, have your child guess what you can see. Chant the following rhyme:

   Can you see what I can see,
   Can you guess what it can be?
   I see something . . . (red, scary, round, etc.)

2. Once your child has guessed, let her take the next turn.

What Is Happening?

Art exhibits do not have to be boring for your children. Encourage your child to use her imagination with this activity. You will also be developing her vocabulary and literacy skills.

ACTIVITY FOR AN INDIVIDUAL CHILD

Age group: 18–40 months

Duration of activity: 30 minutes

1. Find pictures that depict people. Abstract or still-life paintings will not work for this.

2. Ask your child to make up a story based on what she sees. Maybe your child will have a new idea about why the Mona Lisa is smiling.

CHAPTER 5

Art and Exploration

Young children are naturally creative. They love to manip-ulate and explore art materials. They often are more im-mersed in and interested in the process of creating than in what the final project will look like. When a child creates arts and crafts, he is also learning to express himself and is developing emotional control and problem-solving skills. You will find art ideas and projects throughout this book; however, here are some favorites that both you and your child will enjoy.

Coloring

Coloring may be the most basic and common of all art activities for young children. Crayons are inexpensive and easy to transport and to clean. You will discover that you can spark your child's imagination by avoiding coloring books and templates and trying these open-ended ideas instead.

Sparkly Pictures

Liven up your child's coloring projects with this easy idea!

ACTIVITY FOR AN INDIVIDUAL CHILD

Age group: 18–40 months
Duration of activity: 10 minutes

Crayons
Dark-colored construction paper
Paintbrush
Salt water

1. Have your toddler color any design or picture she wants on a dark-colored sheet of construction paper. Remind her to press hard for the colors to show well.

2. Next, let your child use the brush to paint over her picture with the salt water. (Be sure to stop her before the paper becomes too soggy.) The crayons will resist the water. When the paper dries, the picture will sparkle wherever the salt remains.

Tape Pictures

This is a simple way to encourage your child's creativity and fine motor skills.

ACTIVITY FOR AN INDIVIDUAL CHILD

Age group: 30–40 months

Duration of activity: 10 minutes

Masking tape
Construction paper
Crayons

1. Help your toddler tear the masking tape into smaller pieces and strips.

2. Have her put the tape onto the paper in any design that she wishes.

3. Let her color over the tape. Encourage her to cover as much of the paper as possible.

4. Let her peel back the tape to reveal the picture.

Paper Bag Batik

This process will give your child's artwork a unique look.

ACTIVITY FOR AN INDIVIDUAL CHILD

Age group: 18–40 months

Duration of activity: 15 minutes

Scissors
1 brown paper bag
Water
Crayons

1. Cut the bag open so that it forms 1 piece of flat paper.

2. Help your toddler soak the bag in water and then squeeze the water out. Let the bag get wrinkled.

3. The wet bag will tear easily, so open it carefully and lay it flat.

4. Once the bag is dry, your toddler can color a design on it.

Black Magic

This classic activity still delights young children!

ACTIVITY FOR AN INDIVIDUAL CHILD

Age group: 18–40 months
Duration of activity: 20 minutes

White paper
Crayons
Black watercolor paint
Paintbrush

1. Let your child color on the paper with crayons. Avoid dark colors such as black, brown, or gray. Show her how to press hard to make sure the crayon marks are heavy.

2. Once the picture is complete, your child will paint over the entire paper with the black watercolor paint. The original crayon drawing will resist the paint and show through.

3. For older toddlers, or with your assistance: Instead of using watercolor paint, help your child cover the picture with a thick layer of black crayon. (All crayon layers must be extra thick for this to work.) Scrape away patterns or designs using the side of a coin to reveal the vibrant rainbow colors underneath.

Rough Art

This activity will help your child express creativity and learn about textures.

ACTIVITY FOR AN INDIVIDUAL CHILD

Age group: 18–40 months
Duration of activity: 10 minutes

Crayons or chalk
Different grades of sandpaper

Let your toddler explore coloring on the different textures of sandpaper.

Cupcake Crayons

Recycle and reuse old crayons! These homemade crayons are easy for small hands to hold, and they produce bright colors and patterns.

ACTIVITY FOR AN INDIVIDUAL CHILD

Age group: 18–40 months

Duration of activity: 30 minutes

Old crayons and crayon pieces
Muffin tin
Paper muffin or cupcake liners

1. Discard brown, black, and gray crayons.

2. Remove the paper from all crayons. Small fingers may need help with this.

3. Break remaining crayons into small pieces no more than ½" long. Supervise your children carefully to ensure they do not put any crayons in their mouths.

4. Distribute crayon pieces into muffin tins lined with liners.

5. Bake at 300°F until all the crayons are melted together.

6. When cool, remove the new cupcake crayons from the tins—they'll be ready to use!

Painting

There is no end to the number of creative projects your child can complete with paint. Here you will find unique ideas that go well beyond a plastic palette and a little brush. Nowadays, you can find paints that are washable to cut down on the cleanup. Also, you should be sure to opt for nontoxic paints whenever you can. As a general rule, tempera paints are best for young artists—watercolors come in less vibrant colors and tend to run, which might frustrate your child. You will also discover that you do not necessarily need store-bought paint for your painting projects!

Wet Chalk Pastels

Using this new take on an old art material, these paintings will look like a professional artist was at work!

ACTIVITY FOR AN INDIVIDUAL CHILD

Age group: 18–40 months
Duration of activity: 15 minutes

Sidewalk chalk in various colors
1 cup water
Dark-colored construction paper

1. Show your child how to dip the chalk into the water and let it sit for 1 minute.

2. Once the chalk is wet, show your child how to color on the paper—don't press too hard, or the paper will tear. The wet chalk will look like pastel paints.

Sticker Surprise

This activity will help develop your toddler's fine motor skills. Along with or instead of stickers, you can use return address labels, gummed paper reinforcers, or simply pieces of masking tape.

ACTIVITY FOR AN INDIVIDUAL CHILD

Age group: 18–40 months
Duration of activity: 15 minutes

A variety of adhesive stickers
White construction or bond paper
Tempera paint

1. Allow your toddler to choose the stickers that he wishes to use. Stickers with distinctly shaped outlines work best.

2. Show him how to attach the stickers to the paper in any arrangement that he chooses.

3. Paint over the entire paper, covering the stickers.

4. Once the paint is dry, help your toddler remove the stickers to reveal the sticker shapes.

Put Those Paintbrushes Away

Break away from the routine. Let your child's creativity be the only limit to the materials he can use to paint with.

ACTIVITY FOR AN INDIVIDUAL CHILD

Age group: 18–40 months

Duration of activity: 10 minutes

Paper

Tempera paint

Paintbrush substitute(s), such as condiment squeeze bottles, eyedroppers, fly swatters, spray bottles, makeup applicators, cotton balls, cotton swabs, string, tree bark, feathers, straws, pipe cleaners, or toothbrushes

Let your child paint using any number of paintbrush substitutes. He will find that each tool makes a different mark on the paper.

Reverse Finger Painting

This nifty process will let your child preserve his finger-painting creations. You can have him paint directly on the table or onto a cookie sheet for easier cleanup.

ACTIVITY FOR AN INDIVIDUAL CHILD

Age group: 18–40 months

Duration of activity: 10 minutes

Finger paints

White construction paper

Cookie sheet (optional)

1. Have your child finger paint on a flat surface.

2. Press the white construction paper on top of the finger paint and rub—a mirror image of the design will transfer to the paper.

Mirror-Image Painting

No two pictures will ever be exactly alike!
Watch your child's delight when he opens up the paper to reveal the new design.

ACTIVITY FOR AN INDIVIDUAL CHILD

Age group: 18–40 months
Duration of activity: 10 minutes

White or light-colored bond paper
Tempera paints

1. Fold a sheet of paper in half and crease down the middle. Unfold paper.

2. Let your child paint a design on one half of the paper, using the crease as a guide.

3. Fold the paper in half and show your child how to gently rub over the painted design inside.

4. Let your child unfold the paper to reveal his new double design.

Ball Painting

It's like magic—when you open the box, you'll find a picture painted inside!

ACTIVITY FOR AN INDIVIDUAL CHILD

Age group: 18–40 months
Duration of activity: 15 minutes

Scissors
White or light-colored bond paper
Shoebox with a lid
Masking tape
Tempera paints
Shallow pie tins
Ping-pong or golf balls

1. Cut a piece of paper to fit the bottom of the box. Tape it securely in place.

2. Pour small amounts of paint into the pie tins. Show your toddler how to dip a ball into the paint.

3. Have him place the paint-covered ball into the shoebox. Cover the box with the lid.

4. Let your child gently roll and shake the box around.

5. Remove the ball. Repeat with as many other balls and colors as desired.

Sculpting

The more your child can handle and manipulate materials, the more she will enjoy the project, and the more she will learn. Sculpture encourages your child to be creative, to see things in a new way, and to think "outside the box." Let these activities start you off in exploring this art technique with your child.

Yarn Sculpture

Your child will love the ooey-gooey feel of the glue and the yarn as she molds this fun sculpture.

ACTIVITY FOR AN INDIVIDUAL CHILD

Age group: 18–40 months
Duration of activity: 2 hours

Yarn or cord in bright colors
White craft glue
Waxed paper

1. Have your child dip pieces of yarn in the glue to coat.

2. Let your child arrange the yarn pieces onto the waxed paper in any design she wants.

3. Allow the sculpture to dry for a few hours, and then remove it from the waxed paper. You may choose to hang it as a mobile for display.

Three-Dimensional Sculpture

*This project will turn your toddler into a mini-architect!
She will use her problem-solving skills and creativity to make a 3D sculpture.*

ACTIVITY FOR AN INDIVIDUAL CHILD

Age group: 18–40 months

Duration of activity: 10 minutes

White craft glue
Masking tape
Popsicle sticks
Cardboard or poster board in various
   sizes and shapes
Decorative materials such as foil or
   ribbon

Allow your child to glue and tape the materials together to create her own 3D sculpture.

Tissue-Paper Sculpture

Your child will be developing fine motor skills and using her creativity with this activity.

ACTIVITY FOR AN INDIVIDUAL CHILD

Age group: 18–40 months

Duration of activity: 15 minutes

Colored tissue paper
Small bowl
White craft glue
Water
Cardboard

1. Have your child tear the tissue paper into small pieces. They do not have to be uniform in size.

2. In a small bowl, mix the glue and water in equal parts.

3. Show your child how to crumple up the tissue paper into wads. Dip each wad in the glue mixture and stick onto the cardboard.

4. Your child can add tissue wads onto a growing sculpture mound in this fashion.

Papier Mâché

Papier Mâché is fun for all ages. Your young child will love the feel of the squishy paste. The best part is that the only limit to your creativity is your imagination. Be warned: This is a messy project!

ACTIVITY FOR AN INDIVIDUAL CHILD OR A GROUP

Age group: 18–40 months

Duration of activity: 2 days

Old newspapers
1 part flour
1 part water
Mold or form (made from materials like wire, boxes, or balloons)
Decorating materials

1. Have your child tear the newspaper into strips.

2. Combine the flour and water, adjusting proportions to achieve the consistency of very loose paste, like runny oatmeal. You may have to make more paste for progressive layers of your project.

3. Help your child dip each strip into the paste mixture and smooth it over the form. You will probably need to help your child squeeze the excess paste off the newspaper strip before removing it from the bowl.

4. Be sure that the entire mold is well covered with the paper strips. Let the layer dry before applying the next layer. Large or complex molds need multiple layers; small or simple shapes need fewer.

5. Once the sculpture is dry, it will be quite hard. You and your child can decorate it in many ways. Try using paint, markers, and glue with scraps of paper, feathers, or glitter.

Making Collages

There is no end to the number of materials that can be used for collages. Anything that will stick with glue is fair game. Let the ideas below be an inspiration for you and your child to create many variations.

Rice Collage

Your child will enjoy manipulating and gluing the rice. You will enjoy how bright the colors appear. This procedure also works well with dried pasta in distinctive shapes, such as macaroni or wagon wheels.

ACTIVITY FOR AN INDIVIDUAL CHILD

Age group: 18–40 months

Duration of activity: 30 minutes

Rubbing alcohol

Food coloring in various colors

Zip-top plastic sandwich bags (1 for each color used)

Uncooked rice or pasta

Waxed paper

White craft glue

Construction paper

1. For each color, mix ¼ teaspoon rubbing alcohol and a few drops of food coloring in a zip-top bag. Add ¼ cup of rice. Seal the bag and shake well.

2. Spread the rice on waxed paper and let dry.

3. Let your child use the glue to make designs on the construction paper. Sprinkle the rice over the wet glue to create a brightly colored picture. Let dry.

Natural Dye Collage

This activity will produce some very pretty fabric swatches. You may wish to use the resulting collage to make another project from the fabric, such as a kite or doll dress.

ACTIVITY FOR AN INDIVIDUAL CHILD

Age group: 18–40 months

Duration of activity: 10 minutes

Muslin fabric
Natural materials such as berries,
    flowers, and leaves

1. Spread the muslin on the ground. Measure to middle of the fabric swatch and mark the center line so that fabric is divided in half.

2. Working on one half of fabric, help your child place his chosen materials into any pattern or design he wishes.

3. Fold the fabric in half with the items inside.

4. Let your toddler pound the items through the muslin with a small hammer or mallet. Very young children can also stomp on the fabric to flatten the materials.

5. Open the fabric and brush away the remaining materials to reveal the collage design.

Other Art Media

Art is creative. Look around, and you will find many items and materials to use for art projects. Recycled materials often make super art materials. Oatmeal boxes can become drums, and margarine lids make great coasters. Try keeping a box of miscellaneous materials available for your child to create with.

Bubble Prints

You will be amazed at the unique look of this project!

1. Mix a few drops of food coloring into the bubble solution. Pour solution into the pie tin.

2. Have your child use the plastic straw to blow bubbles into the solution. For young children, poke a few tiny holes near the top of the straw to keep them from sucking up any of the bubble solution.

3. Spread a sheet of paper gently on top of the bubbles to make a print.

Homemade Stickers

Does your child love stickers? Now you can make some from just about any image! This recipe is for adults to prepare. You will then have finished stickers for your child.

1. Boil vinegar in a small saucepan.

2. Add the gelatin, then reduce to low heat and stir until gelatin is completely dissolved. Add extract and mix well.

3. Let the mixture cool before painting on the back of chosen images. Once dry, you will have stamps or stickers the child can use by moistening with a dab of water.

Floating Art

Your toddler can create some very pretty and novel pictures using this technique.

ACTIVITY FOR AN INDIVIDUAL CHILD

Age group: 18–40 months
Duration of activity: 20 minutes

Shallow baking pan
Water
Colored sidewalk chalk
Cupcake liners or other small containers
Construction paper

1. Fill the pan with water.

2. Help your child grate the chalk into powder. Place powder into the cupcake liners.

3. Help your child sprinkle the powder onto the water, letting her choose the colors, amounts, and patterns.

4. Have her spread a sheet of paper on top of the water to absorb the chalk design.

5. Hang the wet picture up to dry.

Spin Art

You may remember creating spin art paintings at the local amusement park when you were a child. Here is a simple homemade version to try.

ACTIVITY FOR AN INDIVIDUAL CHILD

Age group: 30–40 months
Duration of activity: 10 minutes

Paper plates
Salad spinner (an old record player
    works well, if one is available)
Markers

1. Push the paper plate onto the record player by pushing the center peg though the plate. If you are using a salad spinner, you may need to trim the disc of paper before placing it into the spinner.

2. Crank the salad spinner to make paper spin.

3. Show your child how to hold the marker to draw on the paper while it spins.

What Remains

*Your child will enjoy squeezing the glue to make different patterns,
and she will be amazed to see her designs glitter and shine!*

ACTIVITY FOR AN INDIVIDUAL CHILD

Age group: 18–40 months

Duration of activity: 15 minutes

Table salt
Glitter
Sequins or small pieces of foil (optional)
White craft glue
Construction paper or poster board

1. Mix salt and glitter in equal proportions. Add sequins if desired.

2. Help your child squeeze designs with the glue onto the paper. Swirls and squiggles look better than large puddles.

3. Show your toddler how to sprinkle the glitter mixture all over the glue design.

4. Shake the paper to adhere all loose glitter mixture possible to the wet glue. Tilt paper to discard remaining glitter mixture.

Crafts

Although crafts tend to be more structured, remember to let your child's originality rule whenever possible. Start with the basic format but do not be afraid to let children make their own alterations and variations to the pattern. So what if they paint the sky yellow, or the puppet has three eyes?

Sun Catchers

Here is a simple craft piece that your child will enjoy making and that you will enjoy displaying.

ACTIVITY FOR AN INDIVIDUAL CHILD

Age group: 18–40 months

Duration of activity: 10 minutes

Hole punch
Clear plastic lid, as from a deli container from the grocery store
String
Colored tissue paper or cellophane
Scissors
White craft glue

1. Punch a hole in the lid and attach string for the hanger.

2. Your toddler can help tear tissue paper into scraps. The cellophane will need to be cut.

3. Have your toddler glue the scraps onto one side of the lid.

4. When the lid is dry, hang in a sunny window.

Shrinky Things

You may remember the commercial version of this craft from when you were a child. Now you can make them at home in a flash!

ACTIVITY FOR AN INDIVIDUAL CHILD

Age group: 18–40 months

Duration of activity: 10 minutes

Scissors
Thin sheets of Styrofoam (such as the butcher trays that come with hamburger or other meats, washed well)
Hole punch
Markers
String

1. Cut the Styrofoam into desired shapes. Punch a hole at the top if you wish to hang the finished product.

2. Help your toddler decorate the shapes with the markers.

3. Microwave the creations for just a few seconds, and you will see them shrink!

4. Thread string through the hole if you wish to hang the finished project.

CHAPTER 6

Sensory Activities

Modern psychological research has determined that flash-cards, drills, and worksheets are not effective ways of teaching young children. Your young child is not able to grasp abstract concepts. Instead, he learns by doing and by using his five senses. Sensory activities help your child learn while he has direct, concrete, hands-on experience with the world around him. This chapter provides all sorts of interesting sensory activities that are perfect for a toddler.

Sand Activities

Sand is a great sensory material for children to explore. It is versatile and easy to find, and it even changes properties when water is added. You do not need to have an elaborate sandbox or table for sand-play activities; simply use a plastic dish bin. Add a shovel, a funnel, and other simple tools, and your child will have all he needs. You will need to tell your child that the sand must stay in the container.

Pirate's Treasure

Your toddler will enjoy searching for the buried treasure!
You may choose to think of other interesting things to bury.

ACTIVITY FOR AN INDIVIDUAL CHILD

Age group: 18–40 months

Duration of activity: 10 minutes

Gold spray paint
Small rocks (large enough not to pose a
    choking hazard)
Sand box with sand

1. Paint the rocks and let them dry.

2. Hide the rocks in the sandbox and let your child dig for treasure!

Roadway

This activity combines the fun of sensory play with your child's imagination.
You can also adapt this activity for any outdoor dirt area.

ACTIVITY FOR AN INDIVIDUAL CHILD

Age group: 18–40 months

Duration of activity: 20 minutes

Flat spatula
Sand box with sand
Small toy cars and trucks
Small blocks (optional)
Toy or handmade mini road signs
  (optional)

1. Show your child how to use the spatula to draw roads and passageways in the sand.

2. Let him create the roadways and then drive the vehicles around.

Sand Squiggles

This simple project is very easy and yet creates a beautiful result.
Add some glitter to the sand for a special effect.

ACTIVITY FOR AN INDIVIDUAL CHILD

Age group: 18–40 months

Duration of activity: 20 minutes

White craft glue
Construction paper
1 small spoon
½ cup of sand
Glitter (optional)

1. Show your child how to squeeze the glue bottle to drizzle a design onto the paper. You may need to put your hand over his to guide him. Fine squiggly lines work better than big blobs.

2. Have your child use the spoon to sprinkle sand all over the picture.

3. Help your child tilt the paper over a garbage receptacle so that the excess sand falls off. Let the picture dry.

Water Activities

Water play is soothing. Splashing and dipping in water is a stress reliever for both children and adults. You may find that your toddler is drawn to water, wanting to play in the sink or puddles. You must always supervise your young child around water. Drowning can occur with even a small amount of water.

Boats That Float

Your toddler will enjoy helping to make these boats as much as playing with them.
You can also use plastic container lids for small craft.

ACTIVITY FOR AN INDIVIDUAL CHILD

Age group: 18–40 months

Duration of activity: 15 minutes

Waterproof markers

Thin sheets of Styrofoam (such as butcher trays that come with meat in the grocery store, washed well)

Scissors

1 sheet white construction paper

1 small drinking straw

Small blob of Playdough (see Appendix A)

1. Let your child use the markers to color and decorate the Styrofoam.

2. Cut a small paper triangle with 2 horizontal slits.

3. Thread the paper triangle onto the straw to make a flag.

4. Place the blob of Playdough in the bottom of the tray to hold the flag.

Glacier Creatures

This is a good opportunity to talk about temperature and melting.
Be sure to choose toys that are not a choking hazard.

ACTIVITY FOR AN INDIVIDUAL CHILD

Age group: 30–40 months

Duration of activity: 3 hours

Small toys
Small clear plastic containers
 (Tupperware works well)
Warm water

1. Place a toy in the plastic container.

2. Fill the container with water and freeze.

3. When the "glacier" is frozen, remove from the mold and add to your child's warm play water.

Water-Play Accessories

Most young children love to play in the water. If you don't have a sand/water table,
a dish bin will work just as well. Your toddler may enjoy simply splashing in the water,
but you enhance her enjoyment by adding a few props.

ACTIVITY FOR AN INDIVIDUAL CHILD

Age group: 18–40 months

Duration of activity: 30 minutes

Sand/water table or a large shallow dish/
 tray
Assorted toys

The next time your child is playing with water, try adding some of these toys and props:

- Plastic or metal tubes or pipes
- Straws
- Squeeze bottles
- Corks
- Strainers or sieves
- Funnels
- Basters
- Floating toys

Natural Materials

Your toddler is naturally inquisitive, and he loves to explore. You don't have to look far to find fascinating sensory materials for him to play with. Don't be afraid to let him or her get dirty—that's half the fun!

Etch a Sketch

This activity can get a bit messy, so you may want to have your child do it outside or over a bin.

ACTIVITY FOR AN INDIVIDUAL CHILD

Age group: 18–40 months
Duration of activity: 15 minutes

Salt or cornmeal
A flat tray with edges, such as a cookie sheet or shoebox lid

1. Put some salt or cornmeal on the tray to a depth of ⅛".

2. Show your child how to use his finger to create designs. You may wish to guide your child in practicing shapes and letters, too.

3. To clear the picture, the child can either gently shake the tray or just smooth over the design with his hand.

Mud Paint

It's okay for young children to get dirty when they play. Why not? Just be sure to do this activity outside.

ACTIVITY FOR AN INDIVIDUAL CHILD

Age group: 18–40 months
Duration of activity: 15 minutes

1 cup of water, or more as needed
Dirt
Old spoon
1 sheet poster board

1. Either find some mud outside for your child to use, or help him make some mud by adding water to dirt. Use a spoon to whip the mud up to a creamy consistency. Add more water if needed.

2. With the spoon, place a blob of mud on the poster board for your child to finger paint with.

Rock Painting

These make handy gifts as paperweights.

ACTIVITY FOR AN INDIVIDUAL CHILD

Age group: 18–40 months
Duration of activity: 20 minutes

Rocks
Poster or tempera paint

1. Take your child outside and help him find rocks for painting. Large smooth stones work best.

2. Let him paint his rocks with poster or tempera paint.

Playdough and Clay

Long before you could buy commercial Play Doh in a can, people were modeling with clay. Playdough and clay activities let your child use her imagination. She can create and destroy as much as she wishes. She can preserve her creation or she can squish it down and start all over again. Don't be surprised if your toddler is more interested in the process of working with this material than she is in creating something specific. You will find many recipes for homemade Playdough in Appendix A.

Playdough Cooking

Making pretend food is just one of many creative uses for Playdough.
You may wish to use older kitchen utensils or pick some up at a garage sale.

ACTIVITY FOR AN INDIVIDUAL CHILD

Age group: 18–40 months
Duration of activity: 30 minutes

Playdough or craft clay
Kitchen utensils

Provide your child with various tools and utensils for cooking up a pretend Playdough meal. Try these tools: garlic press for making pasta, cookie cutters, rolling pin, and measuring cups.

Playdough Textures

Enhance your child's playdough fun by adding texture activities.

ACTIVITY FOR AN INDIVIDUAL CHILD

Age group: 18–40 months

Duration of activity: 30 minutes

Various tools and materials to add texture to the clay

Playdough or craft clay

Provide your child with various tools and utensils for adding interesting patterns and textures to the Playdough, such as a meat mallet, potato masher, corrugated cardboard, or screen or netting.

Mini-Pots

Your child will develop fine motor skills as she explores ways to work with clay.

ACTIVITY FOR AN INDIVIDUAL CHILD

Age group: 30–40 months

Duration of activity: 15 minutes

Playdough or craft clay

1. Show your child how to roll the clay into a ball. Have her use her thumb to create an indentation in the middle and then pinch the sides out wider and higher to create a basic pinch pot.

2. Show your child how to roll sections of the clay into thin coils and then place the coils together to build the walls of a pot.

Bubbles

Bubbles are usually a good choice for entertaining young children. Toddlers especially love to watch them float, to chase them, and to pop them. All you really need is a nice breeze and a vial of bubble solution, but you can enrich bubble play with these activities.

Bubble Catch

Here is a fun and cooperative game that you can play with your young child.
The best part is that you will have pretty pictures when you are done.

ACTIVITY FOR AN INDIVIDUAL CHILD

Age group: 18–40 months

Duration of activity: 15 minutes

Food coloring or tempera paint

2 small containers of bubble solution with bubble wands

2 sheets light-colored construction paper or poster board

1. Add 1 or 2 drops of food coloring or paint to each container of bubble solution.

2. Let your child gently blow bubbles toward you. Hold out the sheet of paper to catch the bubbles. Take turns blowing and catching the bubbles.

3. When you are done, each player will have a picture made by the bubble residue.

Homemade Bubble Solution

Save money and have fun at the same time. You can make as much bubble solution as you need when you need it. Just adjust the proportions to make the amount of solution you desire.

ACTIVITY FOR AN INDIVIDUAL CHILD

Makes 5 cups

Age group: 18–40 months

Duration of activity: 10 minutes

½ cup liquid dish soap

2 tablespoons glycerin or light corn syrup

5 cups water

1. Mix all ingredients together. Don't be afraid to alter the proportions and experiment to create the perfect bubble solution.

2. Store in a spill-proof covered container.

Bubble Bonanza

*This is a fun activity for a hot summer day.
Consider having a bubble bonanza at your next family gathering.*

ACTIVITY FOR AN INDIVIDUAL CHILD OR A GROUP

Age group: 18–40 months

Duration of activity: 20 minutes

Enough Homemade Bubble Solution (see recipe above) to fill a small wading pool about 4" deep

Jumbo-sized wands and other tools, such as hula hoops

1. Fill a small wading pool with bubble solution to a depth of 4". Careful supervision is needed should a child step into it as the pool will be very slippery.

2. Gather large items for kids to use as wands. Try this fun idea: Have a child stand in the center of the pool. Place a hula hoop around her feet and slowly pull it up over the child to encase her in a bubble.

Bubble Tools

You do not need to rely on the traditional wands that come with commercial bubble solutions. When you make your own bubble tools, you can control the size of the bubbles.

ACTIVITY FOR AN INDIVIDUAL CHILD

Age group: 18–40 months
Duration of activity: 10 minutes

Here are just a few ideas for making new bubble wands and tools:

- Twist together two pipe cleaners, then form them into a loop. Dip the loop into the bubble solution.

- Show your child how to hold a plastic berry basket and dip it into the solution and wave his arm around to make lots and lots of bubbles all at once.

- Tie a string to one loop of an unbroken six-pack holder and dip the whole thing into the bubble solution. Wave it around like a kite to get many, many gigantic bubbles.

Miscellaneous Materials

There are many materials that you can use for your child's sensory play. Remember, the most successful activities are ones where your child is directly involved. Perhaps these activities will inspire you to explore some new things with your child.

Shaving-Cream Finger Painting

Toddlers love the feel of the shaving cream squishing through their fingers, and they enjoy the fresh smell as well. If your child can keep the mess contained on the pan, cleanup will be nice and easy.

ACTIVITY FOR AN INDIVIDUAL CHILD

Age group: 18–40 months

Duration of activity: 20 minutes

Nontoxic shaving cream (a nonmenthol variety)
Large baking pan or cookie sheet

1. Squirt a blob of shaving cream on the baking pan in front of the child.

2. Encourage your child to smear and squish the shaving cream around, as he would with finger paint. Some children will dive right in, while others may be very reluctant to do this.

3. When your child is finished, simply wash the pan with hot, soapy water to remove the sticky shaving cream.

Scent Safari

Keep safety in mind while you do this activity with your child. If you use any cleaning, cosmetic, or toxic products, be sure to reinforce the idea that these products are not for the child's use.

ACTIVITY FOR AN INDIVIDUAL CHILD

Age group: 18–40 months

Duration of activity: 20 minutes

Lead your child around the house and find interesting things to smell. Some suggestions include onions, lotion, cedar chips, shampoo, and spices.

Bubble Wrap Fun

Save the bubble wrap that comes with packages. You can also buy quantities of it fairly cheaply.
Bubble wrap, like any other plastic, can be fatal if your child uses it to cover his face.
Always use with hands-on supervision.

ACTIVITY FOR AN INDIVIDUAL CHILD

Age group: 18–40 months

Duration of activity: 30 minutes

Bubble wrap
Scissors
Tempera paint

1. Let your child enjoy popping the bubbles. Show him how to roll the wrap up to pop more than one at a time.

2. Spread the bubble wrap on the ground, and let your child walk and stomp on it.

3. Cut out small squares of bubble wrap. Show your child how to bunch it up and dip it in the paint. Let him push the painted bubbles on the paper for an interesting effect.

Squishy Bags

Here is the answer if you want to plan some great sensory experiences for your
young child but you want to avoid the mess.

ACTIVITY FOR AN INDIVIDUAL CHILD

Age group: 18–40 months

Duration of activity: 20 minutes

2 zip-top freezer bags
Sensory materials, such as mud,
  pudding, or hair gel
Super-strength glue

1. Fill a freezer bag approximately halfway with your chosen sensory material.

2. Glue the bag closed. Put that bag into the second bag and glue that one securely also. Your child can now squeeze and roll his sensory bag without fear of a mess.

Sensory Bottles

Sensory bottles tend to have a very calming effect on young children.
They love to shake them and roll them and watch the contents swirl around.

ACTIVITY FOR AN INDIVIDUAL CHILD

Age group: 18–40 months

Duration of activity: 20 minutes

1 or more (20-ounce) soda bottle(s)

Water

Liquid dish detergent, or

Cooking oil and food coloring, or

Light corn syrup or clear shampoo or hair gel

Small decorative items (such as sequins, buttons, or foil shapes)

1. Choose whether you would like to make a bubble bottle, wave bottle, or slow-motion bottle.

2. For a bubble bottle, fill the bottle ¾ of the way with water. Add 2 tablespoons dish soap.

3. For a wave bottle, fill the bottle ¾ of the way with water. Add 2 tablespoons cooking oil and a few drops of food coloring.

4. For a slow-motion bottle, fill the bottle with corn syrup, shampoo, or hair gel. Add any of the small decorative items.

5. Be sure to seal the bottles so that they do not leak and your child does not have access to small parts that he can choke on.

Music Activities

It has been said that music soothes the savage beast. Whether that is true or not, you will find that music activities will engage and delight your child.

What's Playing?

This activity will enhance your child's listening skills and promote the auditory discrimination needed for literacy skills.

1. Play a variety of instrumental musical selections. Select solo pieces that feature only one instrument at a time, such as dueling banjos, steel drum music, or piano solos.

2. Ask your child to identify the instrument that is playing. Some instruments are easier to identify then others. Start with drums, the tuba, and the piano.

Kazoo

This simple homemade instrument sounds a lot like the real thing!

1. Use the pencil to poke a hole into one wall of the tube, approximately 1" from the end.

2. Let your child decorate the tube with markers.

3. Secure the waxed paper over the end nearest the hole you created. Wrap tape around the lip to keep the waxed paper taut.

4. Show your child how to play the kazoo by pressing the little hole and humming in the open end of the tube.

Little Red Wagon

Start by placing your child on your lap. Position her so that her legs are over yours and she is facing you. Be sure to hold her securely.

ACTIVITY FOR AN INDIVIDUAL CHILD

Age group: 18–40 months
Duration of activity: 10 minutes

Recite the following rhyme and follow the motions:

Bumping up and down in the little red wagon
Bumping up and down in the little red wagon
Bumping up and down in the little red wagon
Oh (child's name) aren't you tired?

(bounce child on both knees simultaneously)

One wheel's broke and the road is bumpy
One wheel's broke and the road is bumpy
One wheel's broke and the road is bumpy
Oh (child's name) aren't you tired?

(bounce child on knees, lifting one knee and then the other)

Try not to let the wagon tip over
Try not to let the wagon tip over
Try not to let the wagon tip over
Oh (child's name) aren't you tired?

(Sway your knees from side to side)

Visual Activities

Young children learn a lot about the world around them through their vision. These activities are sure to engage your child.

Bleeding Tissue Paper

Your child will love the brilliant colors of this project. You can also dye colors onto Easter eggs this way.

ACTIVITY FOR AN INDIVIDUAL CHILD

Age group: 30–40 months

Duration of activity: 20 minutes

Vinegar
Paper cup
Colored tissue paper
White construction paper
Cotton swabs

1. Pour a small amount of vinegar into a paper cup.

2. Have your toddler shred the tissue paper into small shreds. Don't worry too much about size and shape.

3. Show your child how to arrange the pieces of tissue paper on the white paper to create a picture or design.

4. Assist them in using a cotton swab to dab vinegar onto the tissue paper. Be sure they use enough to saturate the paper, but not so much that the vinegar runs all over the white paper.

5. Help your child to remove the tissue paper, leaving behind the brilliant colored picture.

Invisible Pictures

Your child will delight in the magic effect of this picture.

ACTIVITY FOR AN INDIVIDUAL CHILD

Age group: 18–40 months

Duration of activity: 30 minutes

Lemon juice
Paper cup
White bond paper
Cotton swabs

1. Put the lemon juice in the paper cup.

2. Let your child paint on the paper with the lemon juice, using the cotton swabs as paintbrushes. Let the design dry and become invisible.

3. Hold the paper close to a light bulb (without letting it touch). The design will become visible as the juice turns brown.

Invisible Pictures 2

Here is another easy way to create magic pictures.

ACTIVITY FOR AN INDIVIDUAL CHILD

Age group: 18–40 months

Duration of activity: 10 minutes

Bar of bath soap
Light-colored construction paper
Thick beginner's pencil

1. Let your child use the soap bar as a crayon to create a design on the paper. Remind him to press hard.

2. Show him how to rub the side of the pencil over the drawing to make it magically appear.

Shine a Flashlight

Stick with a traditional flashlight rather than a laser pointer that could hurt someone's eyes if misdirected. Of course this game is more fun in the dark!

Shine a flashlight on the child's body parts or on objects in the room and ask your child to name them.

CHAPTER 7

Dance and Movement

Your young child is rapidly developing in many ways. In just a few short months, you will see her exhibit many new skills. From crawling to walking to running, these changes all happen in a short time. Your toddler needs many opportunities to develop her motor and coordination skills. The activities in this chapter will make skill development fun for both you and your child.

Dancing

Your toddler does not have to take lessons and learn fancy steps to dance. Encourage your child to be free with her movements. Let her use her body to express herself. Don't be shy! Why not kick off your shoes and join in the fun?

Dancing Statues

This game will help your child develop listening skills and self-control while she has fun.

ACTIVITY FOR AN INDIVIDUAL CHILD OR A GROUP

Age group: 18–40 months

Duration of activity: 15 minutes

Music

Play music and encourage your child to dance. Randomly stop the music and ask the child to freeze a pose. As your child improves, you can ask her to hold the pose for longer periods of time.

Traffic Light

Your child can learn how to follow directions and develop self-control while she dances.

ACTIVITY FOR AN INDIVIDUAL CHILD OR A GROUP

Age group: 30–40 months

Duration of activity: 15 minutes

Scissors

Construction paper in red, yellow, and green

Paper plates

Stapler

Popsicle sticks

Music

1. Cut construction paper the size of paper plates. Staple paper to plates and attach Popsicle sticks. These are your traffic signals.

2. Play music for your child to dance to. Hold up the different colored signs as she dances. When you hold up the green sign, she should dance fast. The yellow sign means dance slowly, and when you hold up the red sign, she should stop.

Dancing Partner

Dancing with a partner takes extra skill and coordination. Why not pair up your child with someone her own size?

ACTIVITY FOR AN INDIVIDUAL CHILD

Age group: 18–40 months

Duration of activity: 10 minutes

Music

Large doll

Play music for your child to dance to. Provide her with a large doll to serve as her dancing partner. Just about any doll will do, but a large rag doll works best.

Sock Hop

Turn back the sands of time and have an old-fashioned sock hop!

ACTIVITY FOR THE WHOLE FAMILY

Age group: 18–40 months

Duration of activity: 20 minutes

Oldies music from the 1950s and 1960s
Poodle skirts and leather jackets and other timely apparel (optional)

Kick off your shoes and play some oldies to dance to. You can even show your children how to do some of the classic dances, like the twist or the swim.

Hula Dance

Start by making your own grass skirt. Hula dancing is great exercise too!

ACTIVITY FOR AN INDIVIDUAL CHILD OR A GROUP

Age group: 30–40 months

Duration of activity: 25 minutes

Colored crepe paper, streamers, or newspaper
An old belt or ribbon
Masking tape
Recording of Hawaiian music

1. Help your child tear the paper into long strips. Attach them to the belt or ribbon. The more you use, the better the effect.

2. Put the skirt on your child and have her remove her shoes.

3. Play some Hawaiian music and show your child how to sway her arms and hips to the music.

Action Plays

Action plays are popular with young children. They are a great way to engage your child's imagination. Just about any story or rhyme can be adapted. Let these activities serve as an inspiration—maybe you can think of other ways to get your child to act out stories.

Birds That Fly

This is a follow-the-leader activity. Much like Simon Says, the object is to fool the player(s). For younger toddlers, just stick with the true directives.

ACTIVITY FOR AN INDIVIDUAL CHILD OR A GROUP

Age group: 30–40 months

Duration of activity: 15 minutes

1. Call out an animal and an action for your child to imitate. For example, when you call out, "Birds fly," your child should flap his arms like a bird.

2. There are many possible directives, such as frogs that hop, snakes that slither, or horses that gallop.

3. Try to fool him once in awhile by calling out a silly directive. For example, say, "Fish hop." If you fail to trick him, he gets a turn being the caller.

Jack-in-the-Box

This short-action play is sure to get your child's attention and bring some laughter as well.

ACTIVITY FOR THE INDIVIDUAL CHILD

Age group: 30–40 months

Duration of activity: 15 minutes

1. While your child crouches on the floor, repeat the following rhyme in a slow and suspenseful way:

   Jack-in-the-Box, so quiet and still. Will he come up?

2. The child springs up and shouts, "Oh, yes, he will!!"

   HINT: For younger age groups, you can instead play the song "Pop! Goes the Weasel." When the song gets to "pop," everyone can pop up. You may need to cue the children when it is time to do this by yelling, "Pop!" or raising your arms.

Rescue

Engage your child's imagination while helping him develop balance and large motor skills.
You can change the theme of the rescue to suit your child's interest.
Perhaps he can rescue the kitten from the dogs or the princess from the dragons.

ACTIVITY FOR AN INDIVIDUAL CHILD

Age group: 18–40 months

Duration of activity: 15 minutes

Assorted rags and stuffed animals

1. Place a bunch of rags in a small bag or basket.

2. Have your child scatter these around the floor.

3. Choose an object/prop to be rescued. This can be another rag, a stuffed animal, or something else. Toss this object into the center of the others.

4. Challenge your child to walk in and retrieve (rescue) this object without stepping on the others. You might tell him that the dragons are sleeping and that he needs to tiptoe in carefully.

Jack and the Beanstalk

This is a fun activity to do right after reading the classic fairy tale by the same name.

ACTIVITY FOR AN INDIVIDUAL CHILD

Age group: 18–40 months

Duration of activity: 15 minutes

While reciting parts of the story, have your child imitate different parts of the action. Stomp around like the giant and tiptoe quietly like Jack.

Once I Saw a Bird

This cute action includes a nice variety of actions.

ACTIVITY FOR AN INDIVIDUAL CHILD

Age group: 18–40 months

Duration of activity: 5 minutes

Teach your child the following rhyme and corresponding movements:

Once I saw a little bird come hop, hop, hop
(hop around)

So I said, "Little bird will you stop, stop, stop?"
(hold hand in front of body)

I was going to the window to say, "How do you do?"
(wave)

When he shook his little tail and away he flew.
(wiggle rear end, then flap arms)

Exercise Activities

Many adults view exercise as an unpleasant chore. This is not so for young children. You will find that your toddler enjoys exercise just as much as any other movement and dance activities. In fact, she may be even more enthusiastic if she feels that she is doing a grown-up activity.

Hopping Home

This exercise activity will also help your child learn to follow directions. If your child is learning how to count, you can ask her to hop a specific number of times toward the home base.

ACTIVITY FOR AN INDIVIDUAL CHILD OR A GROUP

Age group: 30–40 months

Duration of activity: 20 minutes

Area rug or chalk

1. Define a home base area. You can use an area rug or draw a square on the sidewalk with chalk. Also define a starting place for your child.

2. Your child must ask permission to hop to the home base. Each time, she gets to hop or jump once.

Track and Field

These tried-and-true games have been modified for even the youngest of athletes.

ACTIVITY FOR AN INDIVIDUAL CHILD OR A GROUP

Age group: 30–40 months

Duration of activity: 30 minutes

Carpet square or paper bag
Tape or chalk
Frisbee or beanbag

1. Add challenge to running races by adding hurdles. For the very young, use flat markers instead of raised obstacles to jump over. A carpet square remnant or even a paper bag can be used for this purpose.

2. Masking tape or chalk lines can be made to indicate a long or broad jump challenge.

3. Be creative. An old Frisbee can become a discus, and a beanbag makes a great shot put.

Pumping Cardboard

Toddlers love to imitate. Here is a chance for them to pretend to be bodybuilders.

ACTIVITY FOR AN INDIVIDUAL CHILD OR A GROUP

Age group: 30–40 months

Duration of activity: 10 minutes

Scissors
4 paper plates
2 toilet paper tubes
Crayons or markers

1. Cut small holes in the center of each of the paper plates. Fit the plates on the ends of the paper tubes to make barbells.

2. Let your child decorate her barbells.

3. Show your child how to imitate some bodybuilding poses as she lifts her "weights."

Creative Movement

Who says you need music to get children moving and grooving? Creative movement activities help your child develop motor skills as well as balance and coordination.

Sticky Balls

This silly activity encourages cooperation and helps develop motor skills.

ACTIVITY FOR A GROUP

Age group: 30–40 months
Duration of activity: 20 minutes

1. Have the children all bounce around in a defined area.

2. When 2 children meet, they stick together and bounce together.

3. Continue until all the children are stuck in 1 large ball.

Fun Walk

Children of all ages will want to try this activity. What other surfaces can you think of to include?

ACTIVITY FOR AN INDIVIDUAL CHILD

Age group: 18–40 months

Duration of activity: 10 minutes

Clear contact paper
Bubble wrap

1. Tape a strip of clear contact paper onto the floor, sticky side up.

2. Stick a path of bubble-wrap packing material onto the contact paper.

3. Have your child remove his shoes and socks before stepping on the bubble-wrap path. You may need to hold his hand to help him with balance.

Buzzing Bee

This activity is meant to help children with separation issues. You can dream up many potential variations. For example, you can be the moon and your child can be a spaceship. Or perhaps you are a gas station and your child is a car.

ACTIVITY FOR AN INDIVIDUAL CHILD

Age group: 18–30 months

Duration of activity: 10 minutes

You are the flower, so you sit or stand in one place. Your child is the bee who can buzz all around you and return for pollen!

Flying

This activity is best when your child has lots of room to move.

ACTIVITY FOR AN INDIVIDUAL CHILD

Age group: 18–40 months
Duration of activity: 10 minutes

Chant the following rhyme, and teach your toddler the movements to go along with the words:

The airplane has great big wings (arms outstretched)

Its propeller spins around and sings (spin arms)

The airplane goes up (arms up)

The airplane goes down (arms down)

The airplane goes through clouds all over town.
("fly" around)

Punchinello

*Try this monkey-see-monkey-do activity the next time you have a bunch of young,
restless children to entertain.*

ACTIVITY FOR A GROUP

Age group: 30–40 months
Duration of activity: 15 minutes

1. Have children form a circle. Ask one child to stand in the center as the leader, Punchinello.

2. The children in the circle sing the following song:

    What can you do, Punchinello, funny fellow, funny fellow?
    What can you do, Punchinello, funny fellow, funny you?

3. The child in the center makes a movement. All the others imitate him while they sing:

    We can do it too Punchinello, funny fellow, funny fellow.
    We can do it too, funny fellow, funny you.

4. The child in the middle picks a new Punchinello. Continue until everyone has had a turn.

Using Props

When you add props to movement and dance activities, you enrich the activity and add interest. Also, by using props, you give your toddler further opportunities to develop fine motor skills as well.

Go Team!

No need to have a favorite sports team to cheer on—your child can be a cheerleader at any time.

ACTIVITY FOR AN INDIVIDUAL CHILD

Age group: 18–40 months

Duration of activity: 20 minutes

2 sections of the daily newspaper
Masking tape
Scissors

1. First, create the pompoms. Roll a section of newspaper into a tube shape. Tape the bottom securely and then cut the top half into strips.

2. You may wish to teach your child a simple cheer, such as "Go, team!" or "Two, four, six, eight, who do we appreciate?" Or you can just play marching music and let him swish and swirl the pompoms.

Stick Horse

Watch your child's imagination take off when you help him make and then ride this easy stick horse.

ACTIVITY FOR AN INDIVIDUAL CHILD

Age group: 30–40 months

Duration of activity: 25 minutes

Scissors
2 sheets poster board
Crayons or markers
White craft glue
Yarn
Masking tape
3 paper towel tubes

1. Cut the poster board into 2 horse-head shapes.

2. Have your child decorate or draw a face on each piece of paper. Then let him glue on some yarn for the mane.

3. Using tape, attach the 3 towel rolls together to create the body. Put the 2 heads together back to back and attach them to the "body." Let your child finishing decorating his horse, and he is ready to gallop away.

A Thin Line

A piece of rope is all that is needed to help your child practice balance and coordination.

ACTIVITY FOR AN INDIVIDUAL CHILD

Age group: 30–40 months

Duration of activity: 15 minutes

Approximately 5' of rope

1. Stretch the rope out straight on the ground. Have your child practice walking along it like a tightrope walker. If you wish, you can have him use a balance bar.

2. Hold one end of the rope. Keeping the rope on the ground, wiggle it around and encourage your child to jump over it. If you don't think it will frighten your child, you can pretend that the rope is a snake.

Hula Hoop

It will be a few years before your toddler can use a hula hoop the way it was intended. However, there are many fun movement activities you can still do with this toy.

ACTIVITY FOR AN INDIVIDUAL CHILD

Age group: 18–40 months

Duration of activity: 10 minutes

Hula hoop

1. Lay the hula hoop on the ground. Show your child how to walk around the circle with one foot in and one foot out of the hoop.

2. Hold the hoop vertically and help your child crawl through it back and forth.

3. Join your child, or get a group of children in a bunch inside of a hula hoop. Work together to walk and change directions.

Parachute Activities

Parachute activities are a great way to promote social interaction and cooperation. Children and adults can easily play together in these fun games. You can use a large sheet or light blanket if you do not have a parachute!

Popping Ball

This activity requires children to cooperate to get the ball to do what they want.

ACTIVITY FOR A GROUP

Age group: 30–40 months
Duration of activity: 20 minutes

1 parachute or bed sheet
Tennis or ping-pong balls

1. Have the children hold onto the edge of the parachute.

2. Drop one or more balls into the center of the parachute.

3. Have children work together to get the ball(s) to move. Can they make the ball roll back and forth or around the edge? What do they need to do to get the balls to pop up in the air?

Up and Down

Your child will be developing large motor skills as he works together with the rest of the group.

ACTIVITY FOR A GROUP

Age group: 30–40 months
Duration of activity: 20 minutes

1 parachute or bed sheet

1. Have the children hold onto the edge of the parachute.

2. Instruct them to work together to pump the parachute up and down and to create a billowing cloud.

3. Have them release the parachute when it is fully extended to see which way it will float.

4. Alternatively, after the parachute makes a bubble, have the children squat or sit and tuck the parachute under their bottoms to create a mushroom.

CHAPTER 8

Let's Pretend

As children enter school and mature, their interest in day-dreaming and imagination is often discouraged. We often put the focus on academic skills much too early. Yet current studies are finding that imagination and creativity help children excel at school and help adults fare better on the job. Pretend play is a relaxing and valuable activity for your toddler. Be sure to allow her to plan and play activities of her choice.

Pretend Themes

You will observe some common themes in your child's imaginative play. You can enrich these themes and extend his play by adding props and setting up a scenario for him to explore.

Restaurant Theme

Young children love to pretend to cook and eat food.
As a bonus, you can reinforce manners and social skills while your child is playing.

ACTIVITY FOR AN INDIVIDUAL CHILD

Age group: 30–40 months
Duration of activity: 15 minutes

Table and chairs
Paper plates, cups, and napkins
Plastic tableware
Poster board
Crayons
Notebook
Plastic or real food

1. Let your child help set up the restaurant. Show him how to set the table.

2. Let your child create a menu on the poster board. You can have him color pictures of the food he wishes to serves. Alternatively, he can paste on magazine pictures.

3. Sit at the table and let your child take your order. Supply him with a small notebook so that he can pretend to write down your order.

4. If desired, let him serve you real or pretend food.

Camping Theme

Why not consider expanding this theme with your child? It can be a fun family activity to camp out in the living room for the night. You could even make S'mores in the microwave for a bedtime snack

ACTIVITY FOR AN INDIVIDUAL CHILD

Age group: 18–40 months

Duration of activity: 30 minutes

Small pup tent or large sheet
10–12 small sticks
Scissors
Red construction paper
Sleeping bags (optional)
Flashlights (optional)

1. Set up the tent. If you don't have one, drape a large sheet over a table.

2. Create a fake campfire. Arrange the sticks in a teepee shape. Cut out 2 flame shapes from the construction paper and prop them up among the stick structure.

3. Arrange sleeping bags under the tent or around the campfire.

4. Sit around the campfire and sing songs and tell stories. If your child will not be frightened, turn off the lights and use flashlights.

Medical Theme

Many young children are concerned and often fascinated about injury and illness. The subject of doctors and hospitals is something that your child may wish to explore. You can easily change this into a veterinarian theme; simply add a few stuffed animals and a pet carrier.

ACTIVITY FOR AN INDIVIDUAL CHILD

Age group: 18–40 months

Duration of activity: 15 minutes

Doctor's or Nurse's Hat (see activity in this chapter)
Fabric marker
Old adult-sized, short-sleeved white shirt
Dolls or action figures (to act as patients)
Band-Aids
Gauze or ace bandages
Rubber gloves
Plastic syringe

1. Fit the hat onto your child. Make a lab coat by drawing a pocket and adding a name to the shirt.

2. Let your child put Band-Aids on her dolls and pretend to give them shots to make them feel better.

Props for Pretend Play

Your child's imagination can make a shoe transform into a trailer or a boat, while a margarine container becomes a swimming pool or a foot stool for a doll. Sure, you can buy many toys and props that will add to your child's imaginative play. However, you can engage your child's imagination and creativity in making these simple props as well. Props for pretend play don't need to be elaborate.

Shopping Bag/Purse

Toddlers love to tote their toys around. Here is a fun craft that yours can make.
Always use caution when using long ribbons or cords that could pose a strangulation hazard.

ACTIVITY FOR AN INDIVIDUAL CHILD

Age group: 18–40 months
Duration of activity: 15 minutes

Scissors
Old pillowcase
Fabric paint
12" length of ribbon

1. Cut the pillow case in half crosswise to create a shorter case.

2. Let your child decorate the pillow case with fabric paints.

3. When the paint is dry, gather a small amount of fabric from each end of the opening. Tie the ribbon to the fabric to make the handle.

Doctor's and Nurse's Hat

These easy-to-make props will enhance your child's imaginative play.

ACTIVITY FOR AN INDIVIDUAL CHILD

Age group: 18–40 months
Duration of activity: 15 minutes

White bond paper
White craft glue
Scissors
Bobby pins
Cardboard circle 3" in diameter
Tin foil
Crayons

1. Fold each sheet of bond paper lengthwise into thirds, then fold in half. Let your child glue the folds to form a band. Glue 2 together lengthwise for a longer band. For the doctor's hat, the band needs to fit completely around your child's head. For the nurse's hat, the band only needs to go ⅔ of the way around. You may need to trim off excess.

2. For nurse's hat: Fold up the corner of each end to form a triangle. Reopen slightly and attach to your child's head with bobby pins.

3. For doctor's hat: Help your child cover the cardboard disc with the tin foil to create a mirror. Let your child glue the disc on the front of the band. Secure the ends with glue.

4. Let your child decorate the hats with crayons.

Paper Bag Vest

Your child can decorate this vest to suit her imagination.
It can be a cowboy vest, an astronaut suit, or perhaps a police uniform!

ACTIVITY FOR AN INDIVIDUAL CHILD

Age group: 18–40 months
Duration of activity: 15 minutes

1 large brown paper bag
Scissors
Crayons, markers, or paint

1. If the bag has printing on it, gently turn it inside out.

2. Cut a straight line up the middle of the front of the bag.

3. On what was the bottom of the bag, cut a hole large enough for your child's head.

4. Cut armholes on each side, positioned 2"–3" below the fold.

5. Provide different materials for your child to use to decorate the vest.

Silly Glasses

Now your child can truly see the world through rose-colored lenses.
Remember these glasses are just for play and will not protect your child's eyes from the sun.

ACTIVITY FOR AN INDIVIDUAL CHILD

Age group: 18–40 months
Duration of activity: 15 minutes

Paper cup
Poster board
Pencil
Scissors
Colored cellophane
White craft glue
Hole punch
2 pipe cleaners or chenille stems
Crayons

1. Use the paper cup to trace two circles on the poster board. Leave about 1" between them for the bridge.

2. Cut the glasses frame out in one piece.

3. Cut out an inner circle in each eye, leaving a 1" rim.

4. Cut out cellophane pieces slightly larger than the eye holes. Help your child glue them in place to create lenses.

5. Punch a hole in the far end of each frame.

6. Loop and attach a pipe cleaner into each hole, then bend back the other end for the ear pieces. Be sure no wires are exposed on the pipe cleaners.

7. Let your child decorate the glasses with crayons.

Dolls

Dolls are universally popular toys for your children. Toddlers love to imitate and try out the role that they see the most—that of adult caregivers! Playing with dolls gives your child the opportunity to pretend to be the mommy or daddy and also helps her or him to be less egocentric.

Baby Bonnet Doll

This adorable craft also makes a nice gift idea.

ACTIVITY FOR AN INDIVIDUAL CHILD

Age group: 30–40 months

Duration of activity: 15 minutes

1 little girl's anklet sock (with a frilly cuff)
Cotton balls
Ribbon
Fabric paint

1. Show your child how to stuff the sock half full of cotton balls.

2. Tie the open end of the sock securely. If there is concern that the ribbon could be a hazard for your child, take extra steps to secure it with glue or a few stitches.

3. Fold back the cuff to create a bonnet.

4. Let your child use fabric paints to add on the facial features.

My Statue Doll

Your child can use this personalized doll as a prop in pretend or block play.
For added fun, consider making a doll to represent his friends and members of the family.

ACTIVITY FOR AN INDIVIDUAL CHILD

Age group: 18–40 months

Duration of activity: 4 hours

Instant camera
White craft glue
Poster board
Clear contact paper
Scissors
Air-hardening clay

1. Have your child stand facing forward in a simple pose. Compose the picture so that his head and feet are close to the edge but still in the frame.

2. Let your child glue the photo onto the poster board.

3. Help your child cover the photo with the clear contact paper. The contact paper should overlap the photo by ½" on each side. Cut out the photo.

4. Have your child roll out a piece of clay into a disc the size of a half dollar. This will form the statue's base.

5. Show your child how to stand the photo doll up in the clay base. After several hours, when the clay is dry, your child can then play with the statue doll.

Handkerchief Doll

Here is a cute doll that is easy to make. Skip the ribbons if your child is still putting things in his mouth.

1. Fold the handkerchief in half.

2. Have your child place the ball inside, positioning it at the center of the fold.

3. Secure a rubber band under the ball to create a head.

4. Help your child to gather the fabric from each top corner to form points.

5. Secure each point with a rubber band to create arms.

6. Tie a ribbon around the neck and arm joints.

7. Let your child paint on a face and other features with the fabric paint.

Block Building

There are many ways that your child will benefit from block play. Blocks are an open-ended material, meaning that your child is free to create and imagine whatever she dreams of. When she is building with blocks, she is learning problem-solving and mathematical concepts including spatial relationships, balance, and shapes.

Block City

Help set the stage for many block-building adventures.

ACTIVITY FOR AN INDIVIDUAL CHILD

Age group: 18–40 months

Duration of activity: 30 minutes

Plastic tarp or old plastic table cloth
Ruler
Permanent markers
Scissors
Photos or magazine pictures of different buildings
White craft glue

1. Lay out the tarp to define the city limits. Help your child use the ruler and markers to draw streets, parks, and other desired features.

2. Trim magazine pictures of buildings to glue onto the face of your child's building blocks. A fun alternative is to help your child take photos of buildings in your neighborhood. Capture easy-to-recognize buildings such as city hall, the library, or the firehouse. Only a few blocks have to be decorated with pictures.

3. Let your child enjoy building a cityscape with the blocks.

Stuffed Blocks

Save money and add fun to your child's imaginative block play.
These blocks are lighter than traditional wooden blocks as well.

ACTIVITY FOR AN INDIVIDUAL CHILD

Age group: 18–40 months

Duration of activity: 30 minutes

Newspaper
Empty food boxes, such as those from cereal, rice, or macaroni and cheese
Masking tape
Decorative contact paper (optional)

1. Show your child how to crumple the newspaper into tight wads.

2. Have your child stuff the newspaper wads into the boxes. Be sure to stuff each box to the top.

3. Securely seal each box with tape.

4. If you wish, you can help your child decorate the blocks with contact paper.

Paper Logs

Here is a simple way to create safe logs for building and imaginative play.

ACTIVITY FOR AN INDIVIDUAL CHILD

Age group: 18–40 months

Duration of activity: 15 minutes

Newspaper
Scotch tape

1. Spread three sheets of newspaper on the table.

2. Show your child how to roll the paper into tight tubes.

3. Securely seal each tube with tape.

4. Let your child make a lot of these to use for building, pretend campfires, and more.

Pretend Play Games

Most likely, your child will not need much encouragement to engage in pretend play on his own, but if she does, these activities can get the ball rolling. You will notice that each activity also promotes social interaction.

Act It Out

This simplified version of charades is a great activity for the whole family.

ACTIVITY FOR A GROUP

Age group: 18–40 months

Duration of activity: 20 minutes

White craft glue

Magazine pictures of characters and animals that are easy to mime

Index cards

A hat or other container

Kitchen timer

1. Before the game, glue the magazine pictures onto the index cards.

2. Place the cards into a hat or other container.

3. Each person gets a turn to "act it out." The player removes a picture from the hat and gets 10 seconds on the timer to imitate/mime the character on the card. When the time is up, other players guess the picture.

4. You can choose to let the person who guesses correctly have the next turn or the turns can be predetermined.

Character in a Bag

This is a silly game that will get your child's imagination going!
Be sure to use clothing that is easy to put on and take off.

ACTIVITY FOR A GROUP

Age group: 18–40 months

Duration of activity: 20 minutes

3 paper grocery bags

Markers

A variety of clothing, shoes, and accessories (vintage or costume items add to the fun)

1. Label the bags with markers. You can number them or use shapes or colors to make it easier.

2. Sort the clothing, shoes, and accessories. Place the clothing in the first bag, the shoes in the second bag, and the accessories such as hats and handbags in the third bag.

3. Each person gets a turn to be a character. The player randomly pulls one item from each bag to put on. Once dressed, the person describes who he is and what he does.

Puppets

Puppets are magical. Not only can they breathe life into any story, but they often seem to have a wonderful effect on young children. Many children who have speech difficulties or are shy often feel more comfortable using puppets for expression. A child can project her own fears, wishes, and dreams through the character of a puppet. Make a puppet with your child and watch her imagination soar.

Rubber Finger Puppets

This a quick and easy way to make finger puppet characters for your child.

ACTIVITY FOR AN INDIVIDUAL CHILD

Age group: 30–40 months
Duration of activity: 15 minutes

Scissors
Old rubber dishwashing gloves
Permanent markers

1. Cut the fingers off the rubber gloves.

2. Let your child use the markers to create a face and other features.

Plate Puppets

*Because this project is so simple, you may wish to let your child make
a few puppets and then put on a show.*

ACTIVITY FOR AN INDIVIDUAL CHILD

Age group: 30–40 months

Duration of activity: 15 minutes

Dessert-size paper plate
Crayons
White craft glue
Wooden craft stick

1. Let your child decorate the plate with crayons to make a face.

2. Help her glue on the stick to use as a handle.

Big Head Puppets

*This project takes a little more time and effort, but it is well worth it. Remember to use caution when
using Styrofoam with young children because it can be a choking hazard.*

ACTIVITY FOR AN INDIVIDUAL CHILD

Age group: 18–40 months

Duration of activity: 25 minutes

Scissors
Styrofoam craft balls
Markers
White craft glue
Yarn pieces
Thin fabric remnants, 4"–5" square

1. Use the scissors to gouge a hole in the bottom of the Styrofoam ball. The hole should be wide enough to fit your child's finger and deep enough for her finger to fit in the ball to the first knuckle.

2. Let your child use the markers to decorate a face and other features.

3. Help her glue on the yarn pieces for hair.

4. When your child is ready to operate the puppet, have her drape the fabric over her index finger before attaching the head. The fabric becomes the puppet's body, and the middle finger and thumb become its arms.

Bag Puppets

This is a traditional puppet craft. Frog puppets are especially cute to make.

ACTIVITY FOR AN INDIVIDUAL CHILD

Age group: 18–40 months

Duration of activity: 15 minutes

Small paper lunch bag
Crayons or markers

1. Show your child how to insert her hand into the bag. Her thumb goes below the fold and her fingers go above it.

2. Encourage her to open and close her hand to make the puppet talk.

3. Let her decorate the puppet with crayons.

CHAPTER 9

Games

Playing games is a universal pursuit. Games help children burn off energy, develop social skills, and practice a variety of academic skills. When you teach your child a new game, you are also helping him learn how to follow directions. The games in this chapter are very simple; feel free to adapt them and add more rules and details as your child's skills develop.

Traditional Games

Many games have remained virtually unchanged as they have passed from generation to generation. You will also find similar variations in other cultures. Here are just a few classic games that your toddler may enjoy.

Doggie, Doggie, Where's Your Bone?

Here is another game that is easy to adapt. You can change this game into, "Cupid, Cupid, Where's Your Heart?" or "Baker, Baker, Where's Your Cake?" or "Robin, Robin, Where's Your Worm?" Remember that young children may be uncomfortable closing their eyes, so don't worry about enforcing this.

ACTIVITY FOR A GROUP

Age group: 30–40 months

Duration of activity: 20 minutes

Small toy or dog bone

1. Have children sit cross-legged in a small circle on the floor. Be sure that there is plenty of room around them.

2. Choose one child to be "It." That child crouches in the center of the circle with a toy or dog bone.

3. Tell the child who is "It" that he is the doggie and that he should pretend to nap by closing or hiding his eyes.

4. While "It" is pretending to nap, the rest of the players chant this rhyme:

   "Doggie, Doggie, Where's your bone?
   Somebody took it and ran away home
   Wake up Doggie!"

5. While the children are chanting, remove the bone and give it to one of the children to hide behind his back. All the children should pretend that they are also hiding the bone.

6. When the children say, "Wake up doggie," the child who is "It" rises and tries to guess who is hiding the bone.

7. The child with the bone becomes the new doggie.

Hot and Cold

Help your child develop his listening skills and problem-solving abilities with this game.

ACTIVITY FOR AN INDIVIDUAL CHILD

Age group: 30–40 months

Duration of activity: 15 minutes

Small toy that can be easily hidden

1. When your child is out of the room, hide a small toy somewhere out of sight.

2. Have your child return to the room to look for the object. Guide him with verbal cues. When he is approaching the object, tell him, "You are getting hot." If he moves away from the object, tell him, "You are getting cold."

3. This game is most successful if you are expressive and emphatic in your responses. For example, as your child moves closer and closer to the hiding spot, you might say, "Ooh, you are getting warm. Okay, now you are hot. Wow! When you go by the couch, you are even hotter. Now you are burning up!"

Duck, Duck, Goose

*The beauty of this traditional party game is that you can adapt it for any theme or occasion.
Is it Easter? You can have the children play Bunny, Bunny, Chick. If they're learning about colors,
the game can become Green, Green, Yellow.*

ACTIVITY FOR A GROUP

Age group: 30–40 months

Duration of activity: 15 minutes

1. Have children sit cross-legged in a small circle on the floor. Be sure that there is plenty of room around them.

2. Choose one child to be "It." That child walks around the outside of the circle, gently tapping each child on the shoulder.

3. When "It" taps a child, he also calls out, "Duck." At a random point, "It" selects a child and calls out, "Goose!"

4. The goose must stand up and chase "It" around the circle.

5. "It" tries to run and sit in the vacant spot before the goose tags him. The goose then becomes the next person to be "It."

Cooperative Games

Many games that are played in elementary schools, playgrounds, and birthday parties encourage competition. This is not necessarily a bad thing. However, young toddlers have very diverse abilities, and they become easily frustrated when measured up against someone else. These games have the added benefit of helping young children learn positive social skills.

Keep It Up

You can adapt this activity according to the number of participants by simply adding more balls. You can also use balloons for this activity, but be vigilant with popped balloon pieces because they can be a choking hazard.

ACTIVITY FOR A GROUP

Age group: 18–40 months
Duration of activity: 15 minutes

3 or 4 beach balls

1. To start the game, have participants stand in a circle.

2. Toss a few beach balls into the air.

3. The object is to bat, kick, or tip the balls to keep them from touching the ground.

4. When a ball hits the ground, it is removed from play. The game continues until all the balls are grounded.

Shrinking Island

This game can be played with children of all ages.
It is best for outdoors as it requires a lot of space.

ACTIVITY FOR A GROUP

Age group: 30–40 months

Duration of activity: 15 minutes

Old blanket or sheet or several lengths
   of rope

1. You will need to define the boundaries of the island. You can use an old picnic blanket or sheet. Alternatively, you can set the boundaries with lengths of rope. Be sure that the area is large enough for all the players to comfortably stand.

2. Have participants circle around the island without stepping inside. You may wish to play music. Tell the players that they are swimming in the sea and have them imitate swimming motions as they circle around the island.

3. At the signal (music stops or verbal cue), the players must get out of the sea and go onto the dry land. Once everyone is safe, players can go back in the water.

4. After each round, the island becomes smaller and smaller. To make it shrink, fold the edges of the sheet under, or move the ropes closer together. The goal is for players to work together to make sure that everyone can fit on the island.

Octopus Tag

Also called hug tag, this is a less competitive version of regular tag.

1. Like traditional tag, one person starts out being "It" and tries to tag other players.

2. When a player is caught, he joins arms with "It."

3. This ever-growing mass of children must stay connected and try to move as one to capture the next child.

Group Games

Group games are a great way to help your child develop social skills, as they call for the players to interact with each other. These games are good for times when you have a group of children together. Older children and even adults may also enjoy playing.

Circle Chase

This game will help your child with eye/hand coordination and will also build her cooperation skills. Engage your child's imagination and add to the fun by assigning characters to the balls. Perhaps you can have the dog chase the cat or the bird chase the worm.

ACTIVITY FOR A GROUP

Age group: 30–40 months

Duration of activity: 10 minutes

2 balls (must be different in size, color, or texture)

1. Have children sit cross-legged in a small circle on the floor.

2. Provide 2 balls for the children to pass. Like the game of Hot Potato, children pass objects around a circle. Remind the children to pass objects gently without throwing.

3. Tell the children this is a chasing game.

4. Each ball is a separate character in the chase. Start the balls at different places in the circle. Have children pass the balls until the one "catches" the other.

Hug Rover

This is a variation of the traditional game Red Rover. This version is less boisterous and does not encourage aggression.

ACTIVITY FOR A GROUP

Age group: 30–40 months

Duration of activity: 20 minutes

1. Have participants split into two equal groups. Each group holds hands to form a line. Stand the lines so they face each other.

2. Alternate turns for each side. One side picks on a child from the other side and calls, "Red Rover, Red Rover, will you tell (child's name) to come over?"

3. The child that is called runs over.

4. Rather than trying to break through the line, the child stops when he arrives. The line gathers around and gives him a group hug.

Sardines

This is a variation of Hide-and-Seek. This game usually results in lots of giggles. If a lot of children are playing or the hiding places are small, you can have more than one child hide.

ACTIVITY FOR A GROUP

Age group: 30–40 months

Duration of activity: 45 minutes

Kitchen timer (optional)

1. Designate one child to hide. Have the remaining children hide their eyes and wait. (You can have them count or you can use a kitchen timer.)

2. Once the waiting is over and the designated child is hiding, the hunt can begin.

3. When a seeker finds the hiding child, he quietly joins her in the hiding spot.

4. Each child who finds the hiders joins them. The children may have to squeeze together for all to fit (thus, the name of the game).

5. The last child to find the group becomes the next hider.

Games for Two

Here are some versatile activities that require very little setup and just two players. You can play these games with your child any time you have a few minutes or want to spend a little quality time with your toddler.

Shadow Tag

This game can be played with more than two, but it tends to get too chaotic.
The game must be played outdoors in the morning or late afternoon when the shadows are long.

ACTIVITY FOR TWO PLAYERS

Age group: 30–40 months
Duration of activity: 15 minutes

This game is based upon the traditional game of tag. The difference is that the person who is "It" tries to tag the other person by stepping on his shadow. The other person dodges to protect his shadow. Remind players that this not a contact sport.

Toe Wrestling

This lively game will help your child develop motor skills and balance. It is recommended that one of the players be an older child or adult who can help keep some restraint on the activity.

ACTIVITY FOR TWO PLAYERS

Age group: 30–40 months
Duration of activity: 10 minutes

1. Both players remove their shoes and socks.

2. Hold hands and stand facing your child. Place your feet so that your toes are just touching your child's.

3. The object is to gently pin the other person's toes under your own. Only toes may be used. Try to keep the sole of the foot on the floor. Kicking or stomping is not allowed.

Paper Games

All you need is some creativity to make some cute activities for your toddler to enjoy. Your older child can also play more sophisticated paper games such as Tic-Tac-Toe or Hangman.

Halves

This is a cooperative activity. Older children may wish to try creating animals and other creatures, too. You can adapt this activity for three or four players by simply folding the paper into that many sections.

ACTIVITY FOR TWO PLAYERS

Age group: 30–40 months
Duration of activity: 15 minutes

1 sheet white bond paper
Crayons or markers for drawing

1. Fold the sheet of paper in half.

2. Each player draws half of a person on half of the paper, without seeing the other half.

3. One player draws a head, neck, and arms. Lines must extend a tiny bit below the fold so that the second player can see where to pick up.

4. The second player turns the paper over and draws the torso, legs, and feet.

5. Unfold the paper to reveal your work!

The Clown Says

This is a simple game that you can create that will help your child with following directions and motor development.

ACTIVITY FOR AN INDIVIDUAL CHILD

Age group: 18–40 months

Duration of activity: 10 minutes

Scissors
Paper plate
Poster board
Brad (metal paper fastener, available at office supply stores)
Markers

1. Make a small hole in the center of the paper plate.

2. Cut a small arrow out of the poster board, and make a small hole in the center. Use the brad to fasten the arrow to the plate. Leave it loose enough to spin freely.

3. Use the markers to draw a clown onto the plate; incorporate the spinner as one of his arms. (If your artistic skills are lacking, you can just call the game Stick Man Says.)

4. Divide the plate like a pie into 4 or 6 sections. In each section, either draw or glue on a picture that depicts a movement. For example, a picture of 2 hands could mean clapping.

5. Have your child spin the spinner, then act out the movement that the clown is pointing to. You may need to assist the younger child.

6. Consider taking a few turns yourself. Perhaps let your child spin the wheel for you.

Create Your Own Game

There is no end to the games that you can create! The easiest place to start is to adapt some of the basic sports. A tennis ball and broom can be used for a golf game. Use a beach ball for a gentle variation of soccer. Here are some other ideas to get you started.

Basketball

This simplified version focuses on the skill of throwing and aiming the ball.

ACTIVITY FOR AN INDIVIDUAL CHILD OR A GROUP

Age group: 30–40 months

Duration of activity: 10 minutes

Basketball hoop alternatives (laundry hampers and boxes work well)

Small ball or beanbag

1. Choose various objects that you will use for baskets.

2. Let your child stand back from the basket and try to toss a ball or beanbag in. Keep track of how many shots he makes in a row.

Bowling

Your child will be using his large motor skills when playing this game.
You can set this game up inside or outside.

ACTIVITY FOR AN INDIVIDUAL CHILD OR A GROUP

Age group: 18–40 months

Duration of activity: 10 minutes

6 clean 2-liter soda bottles

1 ball

1. Arrange the soda bottles like bowling pins. If you are playing outside, put some sand in the bottles to keep them from blowing over.

2. Show your child how to roll a ball to knock down the pins.

Fast and Simple Games

Toddler games don't need to take a lot of time or preparation. Count on these ideas to add some fun whenever you need it!

Count Them Up

Players work together in this fun game that helps pass the time.
Younger children who cannot count can still help spot the items.

ACTIVITY FOR A GROUP

Age group: 18–40 months

Duration of activity: 5 minutes

1. One person is the leader. She announces a common item such as trucks or stop signs to be counted by the group.

2. Everyone works together to spot and count the objects.

3. Once the group counts to ten, a new leader chooses a new item.

Fill and Dump

Some toddlers can spend a lot of time repeatedly filling and dumping! Be sure to choose items that are not a choking hazard for your child. Large empty thread spools or bristle blocks work well.

ACTIVITY FOR AN INDIVIDUAL CHILD

Age group: 18–30 months

Duration of activity: 10 minutes

2 or 3 containers
Small household objects

1. Give the child the containers filled with the objects. If the container has a lid, show the child how to shake the container to make noise.

2. Encourage your toddler to dump and fill the containers!

Wizard of Oz

This easy game is a variation of Peek-a-Boo.

ACTIVITY FOR AN INDIVIDUAL CHILD

Age group: 12–24 months

Duration of activity: 5 minutes

A stable curtain or drape

1. Show your child how to hide behind the drape or curtain. You can even have her go behind a shower curtain.

2. Either you or your child may push the curtain aside for the big reveal. Take turns hiding and revealing.

3. When you reveal, you may wish to make a funny face or posture to surprise your child.

CHAPTER 10

Backyard and Nature Activities

There is no better classroom for your child than the world around him. He learns best by direct, hands-on exploration. Abstract concepts are made real when your child can touch and smell and squish the things he is learning about. You do not have to go far to find interesting and fun things for your child to explore. Right outside your door are plenty of opportunities for play and learning. Here are some ideas to get you started.

Gardening Activities

Gardening can be fun for all ages. Your young toddler may simply enjoy playing in the dirt and feeling the cool breeze on her skin. In addition to the wonderful sensory experiences of gardening, there is a special gratification in nurturing something and watching it grow. Let your child help you plant this year's garden. Sunflowers, beans, and zinnias are particularly hardy and grow quickly, making great starter plants for the youngest gardener.

Changing Colors

This is a magical science experiment. Your child can concretely see how plants drink.

ACTIVITY FOR AN INDIVIDUAL CHILD

Age group: 18–40 months

Duration of activity: 30 minutes

1 clear cup of water
Food coloring
Scissors
1 stalk of celery or 1 head Queen Anne's lace

1. Fill a clear glass with water. Add enough food coloring to distinctly color the water.

2. Cut the celery stalk and place it in the glass. See how long it takes for the celery to take on the color of the water.

Pressed Flowers

You will be surprised how easy it is to get a nice result from pressing flowers.

ACTIVITY FOR AN INDIVIDUAL CHILD

Age group: 18–40 months

Duration of activity: 3 days

Your choice of flowers
Waxed paper or newspaper
Wooden blocks or a large hardcover
   book

Arrange the blossoms between layers of newspaper or waxed paper. Press them under the wooden blocks or between the pages of the large book.

Sprout in a Bag

This is a very gratifying activity because your child can see the sprouting process up close.

ACTIVITY FOR AN INDIVIDUAL CHILD

Age group: 18–40 months

Duration of activity: 10 minutes

Zip-top plastic bag
Paper towels
Bean seeds

Moisten the paper towel with very clean hands and slide it into a zip-top bag. Add seeds and seal. Keep towel damp and place bag in a sunny spot.

Bugs!

You may be wrinkling your nose in disgust, but the fact is most children are fascinated with insects. Toddlers are naturally curious and usually only become afraid of insects when they are imitating the reactions of someone else. There are certainly more insects on this planet than any other species, and they are just about everywhere. Don't ignore them. Capitalize on your child's interest in learning. This section includes some fun activities having to do with insects, but the most valuable activity may be to simply provide your child with a magnifying glass and some time to observe the insects all around him!

Catching Butterflies

This fun activity will help your child develop eye-hand coordination and motor skills.

ACTIVITY FOR AN INDIVIDUAL CHILD

Age group: 18–40 months

Duration of activity: 20 minutes

Scissors
Construction paper in various colors
Large kitchen strainer or aquarium net

1. Cut the construction paper into butterfly shapes. Be sure they are small enough to fit into your child's net.

2. Wait for a windy day. Go outside with your child. Toss one or more butterflies in the air and let your child try to catch them with the net.

Butterfly Feet

*Your child will most likely enjoy the sensory experience of having his feet
dipped in paint as much as he likes the end result.*

ACTIVITY FOR AN INDIVIDUAL CHILD

Age group: 18–40 months

Duration of activity: 15 minutes

Shallow pie tin

Tempera paint

White poster board or construction
  paper

Markers and crayons

1. Fill the pie tin with the paint. Help your child remove his shoes and socks, and then help him step into the paint.

2. Have him step directly out of the paint and onto the paper. Help him arrange his feet so he puts them down with heels together and toes pointed outward. (You can spread newspaper to catch any drips.) Have your child step directly off the paper again.

3. Once the picture is dry, your child can decorate the butterfly by drawing in a body and antennae.

Worm Tracks

*This is a great open-ended art project for the child who finds these
garden dwellers fascinating rather than icky.*

ACTIVITY FOR AN INDIVIDUAL CHILD

Age group: 18–40 months

Duration of activity: 15 minutes

Brown tempera paint

Shallow pie tin

Yarn in different lengths and widths

White construction or bond paper

1. Pour the paint into the pie tin.

2. Have your child dip and coat the yarn pieces in the brown paint.

3. Show him how to drag the yarn across the paper to create worm tracks.

Fingerprint Bugs

These personalized insects will help your child develop creativity and fine motor skills.

1. Pour the paint into the pie tin.

2. Have your child dip his thumb into the paint.

3. Help him press his thumb onto the paper to create a thumbprint. He can use crayons to add the head, legs, and antennae.

Coffee-Filter Butterflies

Both adults and children will love these simple and colorful creations!
You can use colored tissue paper instead of dying the coffee filters.

1. Open a coffee filter, and have your toddler squeeze different colored drops of food coloring onto it. The colors will blend together in a beautiful design.

2. Fold the colored filter into a fan shape and help your child insert it into the clothespin. Leave an equal amount of the filter on each side of the pin. Fluff out the coffee filter so that it looks like wings.

3. Let your child glue on the pipe cleaners to make antennae and use markers to make eyes on the head of the clothespin.

Weather Activities

You do not have to go far to explore the world with your young child. The weather affects us all, and it is constantly changing. Regardless of your climate, there are many ways to explore and learn about weather. Here are some ideas for your budding scientist.

Rain Painting

This is a great way for your child to observe how water reacts with other materials.
Your child will also be able to experiment with mixing colors.
This activity is only appropriate if your child will not be upset when the painting is altered.

ACTIVITY FOR AN INDIVIDUAL CHILD

Age group: 18–40 months
Duration of activity: 20 minutes

Food coloring
Paper plate

1. Let your child create a colorful design by putting drops of food coloring onto a paper plate.

2. Have your child take her creation out in the rain to observe how the colors run when the rain falls on them. Be sure to stop before all the color is washed away or the plate becomes too soggy.

3. Return indoors, and let the altered picture dry.

Cloud Pictures

Your child will learn a bit about clouds and explore a unique texture with this project. Older toddlers can first color a landscape picture to use as a backdrop.

ACTIVITY FOR AN INDIVIDUAL CHILD

Age group: 18–40 months

Duration of activity: 15 minutes

Nonmenthol shaving cream
White craft glue
Thick paintbrushes

1. Mix the shaving cream and glue in equal portions.

2. Have your child use this mixture as a paint to create cloud forms. The fluffy mixture will dry and become stiff.

Blown Pictures

This is a fun way for your child to learn about the power of an invisible force such as the wind.

ACTIVITY FOR AN INDIVIDUAL CHILD

Age group: 18–40 months

Duration of activity: 10 minutes

Tempera paint
Plastic spoons
Light-colored construction or bond paper
Plastic straws

1. Thin the tempera paint with water to consistency of watercolor paint. Spoon small amounts of paint onto the paper.

2. Show your child how to use the straw to blow the paint around on the paper. You may need to poke a few small holes in the straw to prevent her from sucking instead of blowing the paint.

Outdoor Activities

Outdoors is often the best and healthiest place for your child to play and explore. When your child is outdoors, he is less restricted. He is free to use a louder voice, to move around more, and to make more of a mess. Toddlers and the great outdoors are often a perfect match.

Leaf Maze

Take advantage of all of those pesky leaves that have fallen on your front lawn.

ACTIVITY FOR AN INDIVIDUAL CHILD OR A GROUP

Age group: 18–40 months
Duration of activity: 45 minutes

Before you rake up all of the fallen leaves in the autumn, clear thin paths through the leaves using a rake or a shovel. You can create a maze or a simple path to follow. If you are energetic, you can also do this with snow.

Picnic Ants

This game can be played indoors or outdoors and will help your child become more observant. You may wish to provide the participants with an old sheet and some fabric paints and let them decorate their own picnic blanket.

ACTIVITY FOR A GROUP

Age group: 30–40 months

Duration of activity: 15 minutes

1 picnic blanket or sheet
Assorted picnic items, such as thermos, paper plates, and napkins

1. Spread out the picnic blanket and arrange the picnic prop items in the center.

2. Have all the children close their eyes. Play the part of the pesky ant: Remove one item and hide it behind your back. (You may also choose one of the children to serve as the ant.)

3. Ask the children to open their eyes and guess which item was removed.

Fun with the Hose

What a great way to cool off on a hot summer day! Like all water activities, adult supervision is needed at all times.

ACTIVITY FOR AN INDIVIDUAL CHILD OR A GROUP

Age group: 18–40 months

Duration of activity: 45 minutes

1. Take and keep control of the hose. Be sure not to spray any child who does not want to get wet, and try to avoid squirting anyone above the shoulders. Never allow anyone to squirt any child in the face or on the head, regardless of the child's age.

2. Try a game of water limbo. Hold the hose so that the water sprays straight across, and challenge the children to duck under the spray without getting wet. Lower the water stream after everyone has had a turn.

3. Hold the hose so water sprays in a long stream across the ground, and encourage players to jump over. To increase the challenge, wiggle the hose.

Nature Crafts

People have been making creative crafts for thousands of years, long before glitter and crepe paper were available. They did without those items, and you can, too. There is no end to the amazing things that your toddler can create using natural materials. The best are those materials that your toddler has found on her own. Let the activities below inspire you to see things such as bark, seeds, and flowers in a whole new way.

Pinecone Bird Feeder

Not only will your toddler enjoy making this project, but the finished bird feeder will attract birds for your toddler to watch and enjoy!

ACTIVITY FOR AN INDIVIDUAL CHILD

Age group: 18–40 months

Duration of activity: 15 minutes

12" length of yarn or twine
1 large pinecone
3 tablespoons smooth peanut butter
1 cup birdseed
Shallow bowl or pie tin

1. Attach the yarn to the pinecone. Make a loop at the loose end for hanging the bird feeder.

2. Help your toddler spread the peanut butter on the pinecone.

3. Pour the birdseed into the bowl. Show your child how to roll the coated pinecone in the seeds to coat it.

4. Take your bird feeder outside, and hang it where your child will be able to watch the visiting birds.

Nature Collection

Here is a fun and easy way for your toddler to preserve all of the treasures she picks up when she is exploring outside.

ACTIVITY FOR AN INDIVIDUAL CHILD

Age group: 18–40 months

Duration of activity: 30 minutes

Assortment of items that your toddler has found outside

1 sheet construction paper or poster board

Clear contact paper

1. Help your child find and collect safe outdoor treasures. Good items include leaves, bark, twigs, and flowers. Watch out for small items that may pose a choking hazard if your toddler still puts things in her mouth.

2. Have your toddler arrange her treasures on the construction paper.

3. Cover the paper with clear contact paper. You will not have to glue anything and it will last a long time. (Alternatively, you can use a larger sheet of the contact paper. Have your child arrange her treasures on one half, and then fold the contact paper over and seal.)

Magic Sun Prints

This activity seems to work like magic. This is a fun way to explore the sun's power as well as shadows and shapes.

ACTIVITY FOR AN INDIVIDUAL CHILD

Age group: 18–40 months

Duration of activity: 3–4 hours

A variety of objects with different shapes

Dark-colored construction paper

1. Ask your child to help you find objects to use to make silhouettes. Flat objects work best. Some good examples include keys, erasers, forks, and shoelaces.

2. Go outside on a sunny day. Have your toddler arrange the chosen objects on the dark construction paper.

3. Leave the paper out in full sunlight for a few hours. The sun will fade the exposed paper to a lighter shade than the paper protected by the selected objects.

4. Remove the objects to reveal the silhouette designs.

Flower Crown

You can make this decorative craft project with your child at different times of the year to showcase the variety of natural materials and reflect the change in seasons.

ACTIVITY FOR AN INDIVIDUAL CHILD

Age group: 18–40 months

Duration of activity: 15 minutes

Paper plate

Scissors

Various flowers, seeds, grasses, and other natural materials

White craft glue

1. Fold the paper plate in half. Cut out a semicircle, leaving a 3" border. Cut spikes and square shapes to a depth of 1".

2. Open the plate. The spikes and squares become the spires of the crown.

3. Give your child a variety of natural materials to glue on the crown for decoration.

4. Let the glue dry before helping your child don the crown.

Astronomy and Nighttime Activities

Nighttime can mean more than bedtime for your child. Just because it is dark, it does not mean that there are not plenty of interesting activities and things to do and learn. Take your child out on a clear night and introduce him to the wonder and mystery of the night sky. Your child will enjoy watching the phases of the moon and if you're lucky, maybe you will spot a shooting star!

Binoculars

Although these "binoculars" do not work, you may find that they encourage your child to be observant and interested in the night sky. Because rubber bands can be a choking hazard, be sure to supervise your child when making this craft or playing with the finished product.

ACTIVITY FOR AN INDIVIDUAL CHILD

Age group: 18–40 months

Duration of activity: 20 minutes

4 large rubber bands
2 squares clear plastic wrap or tinted cellophane
2 toilet paper tubes
Crayons
Star-shaped stickers (optional)

1. Use a rubber band to secure a square of plastic wrap or cellophane over 1 end of each toilet paper tube.

2. Attach the 2 rolls together side by side with the remaining rubber bands.

3. Give your child crayons and stickers to decorate the binoculars.

4. Go outside on a clear night, and use the binoculars to look at the moon and the stars. If you have real binoculars or a telescope, be sure to bring that along, too.

Firefly Firefly

You can play this game during the day, but it so much more fun in the dark.

ACTIVITY FOR A GROUP

Age group: 30–40 months

Duration of activity: 15 minutes

Flashlight

1. All players stand in a circle.

2. Select one person to be "It." That player takes the flashlight and stands in the center.

3. The person in the middle turns around while everyone recites the following chant.
   Firefly firefly in the night,
   Firefly firefly shining bright.
   Turn to your left,
   And turn to your right,
   Pick a new friend and shine your light.

4. The person in the center then shines the flashlight on someone in the outer circle. That person becomes the new firefly.

CHAPTER 11

Literacy Activities

Literacy is the ability to interpret and use written forms of communication. There are many skills that your child will need to learn how to read and write—however, the most valuable thing you can teach your child might be an attitude. Children who develop a love of reading at a young age are more successful readers in school. Take the time now to share books and stories with your child.

Skills and Readiness

Before your child is ready to learn letter identification and phonics, there are many other skills that you can focus on. For a child to be ready to learn to read, she needs to develop auditory memory and auditory discrimination as well as visual memory and discrimination. Memory is recalling and recognizing sounds or images. Discrimination is the ability to distinguish the difference in sounds or images. Your child also needs to learn the symbolic nature of written language—in other words, that words are talk written down. Additionally, building your child's vocabulary will also help her with reading later on.

Do You Remember?

Help your child develop her visual memory with this game.
Try adding more objects as your child matures.

ACTIVITY FOR AN INDIVIDUAL CHILD

Age group: 30–40 months

Duration of activity: 10 minutes

A selection of items from outside or around the house

Blanket or screen

1. Show your child 3 or 4 common objects or toys. Encourage her to name them.

2. Hide the items.

3. Challenge your child to recall and tell you what objects are hidden.

Captions

This is a fantastic way to show your child that words are talk written down.
Your child will be particularly motivated to "read" her own words.

ACTIVITY FOR AN INDIVIDUAL CHILD

Age group: 30–40 months
Duration of activity: 10 minutes

Crayons or markers
Bond paper
Picture book (optional)

1. Whenever your child draws or paints a picture, ask her to tell you about what she created. Write down her words, and create a caption for the art work. Be sure to read it back to her.

2. As an alternative, you can show your child photos or pictures in a book. Invite her to supply a caption by asking her to tell a story about the picture. Again, be sure to write down and review her words.

Does Not Belong

This activity teaches visual discrimination in the same way as the well-known
Sesame Street song, "One of These Things Is Not Like the Other."
You can make many game pieces in varying degrees of complication.

ACTIVITY FOR AN INDIVIDUAL CHILD

Age group: 30–40 months
Duration of activity: 15 minutes

Ruler
Light-colored construction or bond
    paper
Markers or crayons

1. Using the ruler, draw lines to divide each sheet of paper into 4 equal sections.

2. Draw or color identical shapes or pictures in 3 of the sections. Choose a different square on each sheet to leave blank.

3. Draw an item that is different from the others in the fourth square. For example, you may have 3 squares and 1 triangle, 3 red dots and 1 blue dot, or 3 dogs and 1 cat.

4. Ask your child to identify the object that is different.

What Did You Say?

Enhance your child's listening skills and auditory discrimination with this silly activity.

ACTIVITY FOR AN INDIVIDUAL CHILD

Age group: 30–40 months

Duration of activity: 15 minutes

1. Review a picture book or magazine with your child.

2. As you are browsing the pictures, point to different objects and identify them. Ask your child to listen closely.

3. On occasion, intentionally misidentify a picture. For example, point to a picture of a car and say "can," or point to a picture of a boat and say "goat."

4. Have your child stop you when she catches you making a mistake. Ask her to say the word correctly.

Who Said That?

This fun game will help your child with auditory memory skills. You can also play this game using sounds from common household objects that make distinctive noises, such as an alarm clock or telephone.

ACTIVITY FOR AN INDIVIDUAL CHILD

Age group: 18–40 months

Duration of activity: 15 minutes

White craft glue
Photos or magazine pictures of animals
Index cards
Recording of animal sounds that match
   the pictures

1. Glue the pictures to the index cards.

2. Play the recording of animal sounds. Ask your child which picture shows the animal that makes that sound.

Using Books

A love for books and reading is a gift that will last your child a lifetime. Remember books are not meant to be decorations to be gazed at from afar. If you are worried that your toddler will rip or chew a book, buy him books that are made to be extra durable. Let your child have the opportunity to look at books and peruse the pictures. These activities are a great way to use books as a springboard for further literacy development.

Creative Reenactment

This activity will help your child with story comprehension, memory, and creativity. A simpler variation of this activity is to have your child act out specified motions that are mentioned in the story. For example, you might ask your child, "Can you huff and puff like the big bad wolf?"

ACTIVITY FOR AN INDIVIDUAL CHILD

Age group: 18–40 months

Duration of activity: 15 minutes

1. Review a well-known and beloved picture book or story with your child.

2. As you slowly read or recite the tale, have your child act out the drama.

A New Story

Engage your child's imagination and build his vocabulary with this activity.
It is interesting to see the differences between your child's story and the original.

ACTIVITY FOR AN INDIVIDUAL CHILD

Age group: 30–40 months
Duration of activity: 15 minutes

1 new picture book

1. Present a new picture book to your child, and ask him to examine the pictures.

2. Ask him to guess and describe what is happening in the story. For younger children, each picture will have its own tale. You can help your older child link the sequences of the pictures together for a more involved story.

3. If you wish, you can extend this activity by asking your child to draw his own picture to supplement his story. Perhaps his picture can depict what he thinks will happen next.

Story Songs

Here is a fun way to help your child learn story sequence and motivate him to look at books.

ACTIVITY FOR AN INDIVIDUAL CHILD

Age group: 30–40 months
Duration of activity: 15 minutes

1. Share with your children some of the classic songs that tell a story. Some popular ones include "Froggy Went A-Courting," "I Know an Old Lady," and "Three Ships Have I."

2. Select a picture book that illustrates a song that your child knows. Let him read and sing along with you.

Storytelling

Long before the invention of the printing press, fables, myths, and tales were being shared with young children. Each time the tale was told, it was shaped by the teller's interpretation and expression. Today there are literally thousands of wonderful books available for children. But you shouldn't be afraid, once in awhile, to put down a book and spin a yarn for your young child. You have the opportunity to bring a story to life. Use different voices and facial expressions to add interest. Encouraging children to make up stories is a great way to facilitate imagination as well as promote both early verbal and written literacy skills. Get started by involving children as you develop a tale.

Story in a Bag

Here is a way you can spark your child's creativity and encourage her to create her own stories.

ACTIVITY FOR AN INDIVIDUAL CHILD

Age group: 30–40 months
Duration of activity: 15 minutes

5 or 6 common objects
1 paper bag

1. Place 5 or 6 common objects into a paper bag. Suggested items include keys, a bell, a comb, and a flower.

2. Have your child remove the items from the bag. You can either have your child look at all of the items at once, or have her remove the objects one at a time. Help her create a story incorporating these items. For example, "One day a man heard a bell ring. He combed his hair. He used his keys to lock his door and he took a flower to his friend."

3. Consider having your child draw illustrations for her story. Alternatively, write down her story so that you can reread it together.

Fill-in Story

This is a silly activity, like the school-age game of Mad-Libs. Each story will be unique.

ACTIVITY FOR AN INDIVIDUAL CHILD

Age group: 18–40 months

Duration of activity: 15 minutes

White craft glue

Magazine pictures of animals and objects

Index cards

1. Glue the pictures to the index cards, and place them in a hat.

2. Recite a well-known nursery rhyme or fairy tale. Stop at points in the story where a substitution can be made. Ask your child to pull a card from the hat.

3. Substitute the new word into the story for a silly result. For example, "Little Red Riding Hood was taking a basket to her grandmother. Her mom reminded her to take flowers with her also" might become, "Little Red Riding Hood was taking a rake to her grandmother. Her mom reminded her to take kittens with her also."

Next Line, Please

This is a game that can be played by all members in your family.
This a great activity for long plane rides or when you have to wait somewhere.

ACTIVITY FOR AN INDIVIDUAL CHILD OR A GROUP

Age group: 30–40 months

Duration of activity: 15 minutes

1. Each person takes a turn by adding a sentence to the evolving story. The adult may need to keep the story somewhat on track.

2. Your new story may evolve like this:

   Parent: One day there was a bear who . . .
   Child: Lived in a house.
   Parent: This bear was hungry and . . .
   Child: The boy likes toys.
   Parent: So they got together to get lunch and go to the toy store. When they got there they saw . . .

3. Consider having your child draw illustrations for her story. Write down her story so that you can reread it together.

Verbal Games

You can engage your toddler in verbal games in just about any place at any time. These games promote his vocabulary development, expressive language skills, auditory memory, auditory discrimination, and listening skills. Additionally, young children are often very fond of these activities as they feature interaction with you!

Rhyme Time

This activity will help your child with auditory discrimination skills and build his vocabulary.

ACTIVITY FOR AN INDIVIDUAL CHILD

Age group: 30–40 months

Duration of activity: 15 minutes

White craft glue
Magazine pictures of animals and objects
Index cards

1. Glue the pictures to the index cards.

2. Show your child a card, and have him identify the picture.

3. Ask him to generate rhymes for the picture. Not all rhymes have to be real words. For example, if the picture is of a cat, potential rhymes could include bat, fat, gat, lat, and mat.

Echo Echo

Your child's auditory memory will improve rapidly as he plays this game. Using words with similar sounds will also help him with auditory discrimination. There are also many popular songs that feature echoes.

ACTIVITY FOR AN INDIVIDUAL CHILD

Age group: 18–40 months
Duration of activity: 15 minutes

1. Ask your child to repeat what you say to him.

2. Start very slowly and simply and gradually add complexity. You can add complexity by using nonsense words, words that sound alike, or by simply extending the length of your message.

Play Phone

What better way to get your child talking and build vocabulary than to have him use the phone?

ACTIVITY FOR AN INDIVIDUAL CHILD

Age group: 18–40 months
Duration of activity: 15 minutes

Toy phone (or unplugged real one)

Encourage your child to pretend to call a friend or loved one. Your child will probably not need much encouragement. Don't be surprised if he carries on full conversations, imagining the other person's part.

Flannel-Board Activities

Discover what many preschool teachers already know, that flannel boards are a great way to engage young children in a story. You can make the story more concrete and involve the child directly. You may choose to buy a ready-made felt-board kit, or you can make one yourself with some felt scraps and Velcro.

Story Board

Here is a fun way to bring a story to life.
You can also use nursery rhymes and simple poems with this activity.

ACTIVITY FOR AN INDIVIDUAL CHILD

Age group: 30–40 months
Duration of activity: 15 minutes

Scissors
Felt
Flannel board
White craft glue

1. Choose a well-known simple story to illustrate.

2. Cut out felt pieces in the shapes of the main characters and props. For the story "The Three Billy Goats Gruff," you would need three goats, a troll, and a bridge.

3. Recite the story, and have your child glue the pieces onto the flannel board to match the action of the tale.

Outline Match

Your toddler will have fun while learning about shapes and developing skills in visual discrimination and problem solving.

ACTIVITY FOR AN INDIVIDUAL CHILD

Age group: 30–40 months
Duration of activity: 15 minutes

Scissors
Felt
Flannel or felt board
White chalk

1. Cut out a variety of shapes and figures from the felt.

2. Place the pieces on the flannel board and outline them with the chalk.

3. Trim the shapes to make them slightly smaller than the outlines.

4. Challenge your child to fit the pieces inside the outlines.

Making Books

What better way to help your child develop a love of books than to have her create a book of her own? You can bet your child will be more motivated to read when she is reading her own words. As your child grows, you may wish to continue this practice. Books can become more involved and may feature ABCs or something of special interest to the child, such as family pets or hobbies. This activity will also help your child understand the symbolic use of words.

Scrapbook

Scrapbooking has become a very popular hobby.
Why not let your toddler create a scrapbook of her own?

ACTIVITY FOR AN INDIVIDUAL CHILD

Age group: 30–40 months
Duration of activity: 15 minutes

Photographs
Mementos and souvenirs
Scrapbook / photo album
Scissors
Index cards
Markers

1. Let your child select the photos and mementos she wants to include in her scrapbook.

2. Cut the index cards into strips to use as labels.

3. Encourage your child to dictate a label or even a short commentary for each item in the book. Attach the label to the scrapbook.

Texture Book

Your young child will delight in creating a book that she can handle and feel whenever she wants.

ACTIVITY FOR AN INDIVIDUAL CHILD

Age group: 18–30 months
Duration of activity: 20 minutes

Hole punch
Sheets of thin craft foam
Notebook ring
A variety of fabrics with different
    textures
White craft glue

1. Punch a hole in the top left corner of each foam sheet.

2. Attach the sheets with the notebook ring.

3. Have your child choose fabric scraps to use in the book. Suggested materials include corduroy, denim, burlap, silk, wool, and nylon.

4. Help your child glue a fabric swatch to each page of the book.

5. "Read" the book with your child by encouraging her to touch the materials. Guide her, using words to describe what she feels.

CHAPTER 12

All about Me

One of your child's first stops in his exploration of the world around him is learning all about himself. This is an exciting time, when your young toddler starts to develop into an individual. He is becoming more aware of himself as an entity separate from you and is becoming more independent as well. You can use these activities to help promote your child's growth and build his competence and confidence.

Learning-about-Family Activities

Your child's first relationships are with her family. By learning about families in general and about her family specifically, your toddler will learn how people interact with, love, and support each other. She will also learn her role in your family. You will notice that some of the activities in this chapter involve other family members. This is a great way to build family cohesion with your toddler as she learns.

Family Tree

Help your child make a physical representation of your family.
This project is even more fun if everyone in the family participates.

ACTIVITY FOR AN INDIVIDUAL CHILD

Age group: 30–40 months

Duration of activity: 30 minutes

1 large sheet poster board
Thin tree branch (optional)
White craft glue
Crayons
Small photos of individual family
   members

1. On the poster board, either glue on the tree branch or use crayons to draw the tree. Help your child use crayons to draw in branches for each family member.

2. Glue the photos on the branches. Show your child how to place senior family members such as grandparents and parents on the upper branches. If you wish, label each photo.

Big Feet, Little Feet

This activity will help your child learn about sizes and comparison. You may wish to do this activity with hands as well. If you have a cooperative cat or dog in the family, you can include it, too.

ACTIVITY FOR AN INDIVIDUAL CHILD

Age group: 18–40 months

Duration of activity: 30 minutes

Construction paper
Markers
Scissors
Crayons

1. Have each family member place his or her feet on the construction paper. Help your child trace around the feet with a marker.

2. Cut the "feet" out and label them.

3. Show your child how to compare the sizes of family feet. Can she guess which outline belongs to each family member?

4. Let your child decorate the feet with crayons.

I Know Your Nose

Can your child identify other family members by just looking at a nose or other facial feature? This activity develops visual discrimination and problem-solving skills.

ACTIVITY FOR AN INDIVIDUAL CHILD

Age group: 18–40 months

Duration of activity: 15 minutes

Scissors
Close-up portraits of family members, including one of your toddler
White craft glue
Index cards

1. Cut out each family member's facial features (eyes, nose, and mouth).

2. Glue all of the eye sets to one index card, all of the noses on another, and the mouths on a third.

3. For each card, challenge your toddler to identify the owner of the facial features.

4. To extend this activity, omit the step of gluing the pictures onto the index cards; instead, tape them on temporarily. Let your child remove them and create a new person by jumbling the facial features into a new face.

Hiding Family

This traditional finger play is a great way to help your toddler learn about family titles while she develops fine motor control.

ACTIVITY FOR AN INDIVIDUAL CHILD

Age group: 18–40 months
Duration of activity: 5 minutes

1. Show your child how to hide her hands behind her back.

2. Teach her this song with the corresponding motions. Use the tune "Frère Jacques."

   Where's the father? Where's the father?

   Here I am

   (extend one hand with thumb out)
   Here I am.

   (repeat motion with other hand)
   How are you today, dear?

   Very well, I thank you.

   (wiggle fingers as if they were speaking to each other)
   Time to hide.

   (put hand behind the back)
   Time to hide.

   (repeat motion with other hand)

   Additional verses:

   Where is the mother? (index finger)

   Where is the brother? (middle finger)

   Where is the sister? (ring finger)

   Where is the baby? (pinkie finger)

   Where is the family? (all fingers)

Learning-about-My-Body Activities

From the moment your child discovered his own toes, he has been learning about his body and how it works. Toddlers are often eager to learn about the body and will show pride and share their knowledge as they explore and identify their body parts.

My Hands

This fun activity will help your child learn about different parts of his body and will enhance his verbal skills, too.

ACTIVITY FOR AN INDIVIDUAL CHILD

Age group: 18–40 months

Duration of activity: 5 minutes

Teach your child the following rhyme and encourage him to act out the words:

My hands upon my head I'll place
On my shoulders, on my face.
At my waist, and by my side.
I will raise them way up high
And then make my fingers fly.
Then I will clap one, two, three,
Then rest them gently on my knee.

Riddle Me This

Promote your child's problem-solving skills with this game. You can play it anywhere, any time.

ACTIVITY FOR AN INDIVIDUAL CHILD

Age group: 30–40 months

Duration of activity: 10 minutes

1. Ask your child to try to guess the answer to simple riddles. All the answers should be a part of the body. Here are a few examples:

    You use me to hold a crayon. (Hand)
    I am the part of the body that eats food. (Mouth)

2. Vary the complexity according to your toddler's ability. You may even encourage him to think of some riddles for you.

Build a Person

Your child develops his fine motor skills and problem-solving ability as he pieces together a person.

ACTIVITY FOR AN INDIVIDUAL CHILD

Age group: 18–40 months

Duration of activity: 30 minutes

Body shapes cut from construction paper, or magazine pictures of body parts
White craft glue
1 piece of poster board

1. If you are using construction paper pieces, be sure to keep them very simple, such as a torso, arms, legs, and head. If you use magazine pictures, consider involving your child in the search for appropriate clippings.

2. Assist your child in gluing the body-part pieces to the poster board to create a person.

All about Me

Your toddler will delight in seeing a life-size copy of himself.
If you cannot get a large enough roll of paper, you can use an old sheet and fabric paints instead.

ACTIVITY FOR AN INDIVIDUAL CHILD

Age group: 18–40 months
Duration of activity: 15 minutes

Large roll of butcher paper
Markers
Crayons

1. Have your child lay flat on his back on the paper. Experiment with different positions of his arms and legs. Trace an outline around his body.

2. Point out to your child the different body parts on the outline. Label them if you wish.

3. Let your child color the outline with crayons.

Touchy Touchy

This silly game will help your child learn body-part identification.
(For older children, you may wish to talk about private body parts that other people should not touch.)
This becomes like a simple game of Twister!

ACTIVITY FOR AN INDIVIDUAL CHILD

Age group: 18–40 months
Duration of activity: 15 minutes

1. Call out different parts of the body. You touch that part on your child while he touches that part of you.

2. Let your older child take a turn calling out body parts, too.

I Am Special

As your toddler grows, she develops a self-concept. She is becoming increasingly aware that she is an individual person with her own tastes, interests, and personality. Early on, she will have experiences that will shape her self-concept and esteem. Both directly and indirectly, she will be receiving messages about her worth and competence. You can plan specific activities that will reinforce the message that she is indeed very special.

Self-Portrait

Have your toddler do a self-portrait a few times a year.
This is a great way to measure her progress in self-image as well as motor control.

ACTIVITY FOR AN INDIVIDUAL CHILD

Age group: 18–40 months

Duration of activity: 15 minutes

Light-colored construction or bond paper
Crayons
White craft glue (optional)
Yarn and fabric scraps (optional)

1. Provide your child with a paper and crayons to create a self-portrait.

2. If desired, let her glue on yarn for hair and scraps of fabric for clothes.

All-about-Me Book

Your child can create a lasting memory. She will enjoy "reading" it as much as she did creating it. You can bind the pages together with a stapler or by punching holes in the sides and attaching the pages with a yarn bow.

ACTIVITY FOR AN INDIVIDUAL CHILD

Age group: 18–40 months

Duration of activity: 45 minutes

Markers
Light-colored construction or bond
  paper
Magazines
Scissors
White craft glue

1. Label each page of your child's book with a title, such as "My Favorite Foods" or "Toys I Play With."

2. Help your child find appropriate pictures in the magazines to cut out and paste onto the pages.

I Go to Pieces

Enhance your child's self-esteem with this project. This also makes a great gift for grandparents. Simply put it into a box labeled, "I love you to pieces."

ACTIVITY FOR AN INDIVIDUAL CHILD

Age group: 18–40 months

Duration of activity: 45 minutes

White craft glue
Photograph of your child, enlarged to 8"
  x 10" or larger
Poster board cut to same size as photo
Clear contact paper
Scissors

1. Glue the photo of your child onto the poster board and cover with the clear contact paper.

2. Cut the photo into puzzle pieces. You can make the puzzle simple with fewer pieces, or more complex with more pieces.

3. Give your child the new personalized puzzle to complete.

Monkey in the Mirror

Young children are often fascinated by mirrors and their own images.
Your toddler may enjoy simply making silly faces in the mirror.
Don't worry—the dry-erase ink is easy to remove with a glass cleaner and a paper towel.

ACTIVITY FOR AN INDIVIDUAL CHILD

Age group: 30–40 months

Duration of activity: 10 minutes

Mirror
Dry-erase markers

Have your child stand in front of the mirror and show her how she can use the markers to trace over her image. She may also want to give herself a hat or other accessories.

How I Grow

Your child will be aware that he is small. He will probably start to show an interest in being a big boy as he becomes more independent and competent. You can capitalize on his interest with these activities. These activities will also be teaching your child the math and science concepts of comparison, growth, and measurement.

I Am Smaller Than

Here is a concrete way to show your child how his size compares with others.

ACTIVITY FOR AN INDIVIDUAL CHILD

Age group: 18–40 months

Duration of activity: 20 minutes

Yarn
Scissors

1. Have your toddler stand with his back to a wall. Run the yarn from his head to his toes, and cut it to the length of his body.

2. Show your child that the yarn piece represents his height. Take the yarn and hold it up to yourself and other family members to compare. You may also wish to compare the yarn with household furniture and other things in his environment. Is he taller than the fence? Is he shorter than the refrigerator?

As I Grow

Your child will enjoy reviewing photos of himself. You may also wish to share photos of yourself from when you were growing up.

ACTIVITY FOR AN INDIVIDUAL CHILD

Age group: 18–40 months

Duration of activity: 10 minutes

Photos of your child at different ages

Assist your child in putting the photos in sequence from youngest to oldest. Point out to your child the physical differences that are observable in the photos.

Five-Senses Activities

Your toddler relies on her senses to learn about the world around her. She is not yet able to learn about abstract concepts. She only knows about the concrete, real world, things that she has experienced directly. Engage your toddler's senses, and you engage her mind!

Name That Sound

This activity will help your child use problem-solving skills. She will also be practicing auditory memory and discrimination skills that will help her later with reading.

ACTIVITY FOR AN INDIVIDUAL CHILD

Age group: 30–40 months

Duration of activity: 10 minutes

Recording of various common sounds (such as dog barking, phone ringing, or alarm clock beeping)

Play the tape and have your child guess what is making the sounds that she hears.

What Is That Smell?

Stimulate your child's senses with this activity, which also helps develop vocabulary.

ACTIVITY FOR AN INDIVIDUAL CHILD

Age group: 30–40 months

Duration of activity: 10 minutes

Cotton balls

Items from around the house with
distinctive pleasant odors (such as
vanilla extract, lemon juice, crushed
garlic, perfume, or ground cinnamon)

1. Saturate each cotton ball in a different substance.

2. Have your child try to describe the scent and guess its source.

Smelly Tacky Paintings

This is a fun project that will let your child explore different scents and textures while being creative.

ACTIVITY FOR AN INDIVIDUAL CHILD

Age group: 18–40 months

Duration of activity: 20 minutes

Spoon

Water

Light-colored construction or bond
paper

Different flavors of Jell-O (dark colors
work best)

1. Help your child spoon a small amount of water onto the paper.

2. Let your child sprinkle the Jell-O powder on the wet patches.

3. Your child can then finger paint with these colors. She needs to be gentle so as not to rub through the paper. As she works, she will find that the consistency of the "paint" changes from gritty to sticky to slimy.

Fuzzy Hand

Young children like to touch things, and this activity provides an opportunity to explore different textures.

ACTIVITY FOR AN INDIVIDUAL CHILD

Age group: 18–40 months

Duration of activity: 20 minutes

1 large sheet poster board
Pencil
Scissors
White craft glue
Various fabric scraps with different
   textures (such as burlap, satin, cotton,
   or corduroy)

1. Place your child's hands on the poster board. Trace around them, and then cut out multiple paper hands.

2. Let your child glue the various materials onto the hands. Talk about how each hand feels.

Learning to Be Safe and Healthy

It is never too early to teach your child about keeping healthy. Although you can do activities with him, remember that your child will learn by your example. If you want your child to make good food choices, be mindful of what you eat. If you want your child to brush his teeth, be sure to brush yours as well. As your child matures, you will be able to use direct instruction more and more. Keep in mind that to be effective, these activities need to be interesting and fun for your child so that he wants to continue them on his own.

Paper-Plate Meals

Help your child learn about nutrition and balanced meals with this activity.
You may wish to introduce the concept of the basic food groups here.

ACTIVITY FOR AN INDIVIDUAL CHILD

Age group: 30–40 months

Duration of activity: 30 minutes

Magazines
Scissors
White craft glue
Paper plates

1. Go through the magazines with your child and help him select food pictures that he wants to include in his "meal."

2. Assist your child in tearing or cutting out the selected pictures.

3. Show your child how to glue the food onto me the plate to create a meal. Your child may enjoy doing a separate plate for each meal of the day.

Feed Me!

Here is a fun way to help your child start to make healthy food choices.
Instead of making the head, you can purchase a bean-bag target face for the same purpose.

ACTIVITY FOR AN INDIVIDUAL CHILD

Age group: 30–40 months

Duration of activity: 45 minutes

Scissors
1 large sheet poster board or cardboard
Markers and crayons
Food pictures cut from magazines

1. Cut a large head (approximately the size of a beach ball) out of poster board. Cut out a hole for the mouth.

2. Have your child help you decorate the head.

3. Provide your child with a variety of magazine clippings of food pictures. Be sure to have a wide selection of both nutritious and junk foods. Ask your child to feed the head with only those foods that are nutritious.

Sparkle Germs

Young children are often resistant to washing their hands. It is hard for them to understand things that they cannot see. Here is a concrete way to teach them about germs and the importance of washing hands.

ACTIVITY FOR AN INDIVIDUAL CHILD

Age group: 30–40 months
Duration of activity: 10 minutes

Craft glitter

1. Sprinkle a bit of glitter onto your child's hands. Explain that these glitter specks are like germs, which can make them sick. The germs are very small and they stick to you and get passed along.

2. Have your child touch different surfaces and shake hands with other people. Show him how the germs (glitter) spread.

3. Have your child wash his hands and see how the germs are washed away.

Brush the Tooth

It is never too early to teach your child about the importance of good dental hygiene.

ACTIVITY FOR AN INDIVIDUAL CHILD

Age group: 18–40 months
Duration of activity: 10 minutes

Scissors
1 sheet yellow construction paper
An old toothbrush
White tempera paint

1. Cut a tooth shape from the construction paper.

2. Talk with your child about teeth and how when they are not brushed, they can develop decay and turn yellow.

3. Let him use the toothbrush to paint the tooth with pretend toothpaste (white paint).

CHAPTER 13

For Special Needs Toddlers

All children have the capacity to learn, grow and have fun! Each child is unique and part of your challenge is to find activities that meet their individual needs. When caring for a child with special needs, you may find that you can adapt many activities to suit the child.

For Children with Sensory Disabilities

These activities are especially beneficial for children with sensory integration disorders. They will help stimulate your child's tactile awareness and body and space perception.

Handprint Octopus

Your child may enjoy creating an entire underwater scene around the handprint octopus, so have her do this on a large sheet of paper where she can color in a background scene.

ACTIVITY FOR AN INDIVIDUAL CHILD

Age group: 18–40 months

Duration of activity: 15 minutes

Tempera paint
Shallow pie tin
Large sheet of blue construction paper or poster board
Markers or crayons

1. Pour the paint into the tin. Help your child dip her hand into the paint and then press it firmly onto the paper. Have her repeat this process with her other hand. Be sure that her hand prints overlap, with the fingers spread out in opposite directions.

2. Once the paint is dry, she can use the markers to add facial features and details.

Silhouette

Once you create your child's silhouette picture, you may wish to do one for the entire family. You may also wish to create a traditional silhouette by cutting the outline from black construction paper.

ACTIVITY FOR AN INDIVIDUAL CHILD

Age group: 30–40 months

Duration of activity: 25 minutes

Masking tape
Large sheet of white paper
Chair
Bright light (a clip-on office lamp works well)
Dark-colored marker
Crayons

1. Tape the paper onto a flat wall.

2. Seat your child sideways on the chair with the lamp behind her. Put the chair far enough from the wall that your child's shadow fills the paper.

3. Trace around your child's silhouette using the marker.

4. Remove the paper and allow your child to decorate her profile.

Paint a Song

This activity will help your child with emotional expression and creativity.

ACTIVITY FOR AN INDIVIDUAL CHILD

Age group: 18–40 months

Duration of activity: 15 minutes

Large sheet poster board
Tempera paint
Pie tins
Paintbrushes
Variety of music recordings

1. Set up the paper and paints for your child to create.

2. Play music of differing tempos and moods. Ask your child to listen to the music and let the music guide the way she paints. For example, when listening to a waltz, she may paint with slow, sweeping strokes.

For Children with Autism

Children that are diagnosed with an Autism Spectrum Disorder need experiences and encouragement interacting with other people. These activities encourage both social and verbal skills.

Little Mouse

This is a tickle and cuddle activity. Be aware that some children do not like to be tickled!

ACTIVITY FOR AN INDIVIDUAL CHILD

Age group: 18–40 months
Duration of activity: 15 minutes

Recite the following poem while using your fingers to trace the path described.

Hurry hurry little mouse
Starts down at your toes.
Hurry hurry little mouse
Past your knees he goes.
Hurry hurry little mouse
Past where your tummy is.
Hurry hurry little mouse
Gives you a mousy kiss.

(blow raspberry on child's stomach)

Mouth Music

Your young child loves to imitate, and this is a great way for him to learn!

ACTIVITY FOR AN INDIVIDUAL CHILD

Age group: 18–30 months
Duration of activity: 10 minutes

Lose your own inhibitions and demonstrate many sounds that you can make. Encourage your child to join in. Suggested actions include kissing the air, making raspberries with your tongue, humming, cooing, blowing through your lips, clicking your tongue, squeaking, and growling.

Teddy Bear, Teddy Bear

This is an easy rhyme for your child to learn. Don't be afraid to make up verses of your own.

ACTIVITY FOR AN INDIVIDUAL CHILD

Age group: 18–40 months
Duration of activity: 15 minutes

Teach this rhyme and corresponding movements to your child:

Teddy bear, teddy bear turn around.
Teddy bear teddy bear touch the ground.
Teddy bear teddy bear hug me tight.
Teddy bear teddy bear say goodnight.

For Children with Mobility Disabilities

Remember to adapt activities to meet your child's needs or challenges. These activities can be done in different ways and don't require a child to be ambulatory.

Roll Over

Your child will need a lot of room for this activity. A grassy spot in the yard would work well.

ACTIVITY FOR AN INDIVIDUAL CHILD

Age group: 18–30 months
Duration of activity: 10 minutes

Have your child lie down with her arms at her sides. Teach her the following rhyme. Encourage her to roll over when the movement is called for in the song:

There were five in a bed and the little one said,
"Roll over, roll over."
So they all rolled over, and one fell out.
There were four in the bed and the little one said,
"Roll over, roll over."
So they all rolled over, and one fell out.
(Continue to one)
Only the little one was left in the bed he said,
"Good night, sleep tight."

Row the Boat

Young children learn that they must take turns for this activity to work. Provide them a soft surface so that they can get exuberant without getting hurt. Younger children can work with a more mature partner.

ACTIVITY FOR TWO CHILDREN

Age group: 30–40 months
Duration of activity: 15 minutes

1. Seat children on the floor facing each other, with legs outstretched.

2. Have one child rest her legs over the other's. Once they are positioned, have the children hold hands.

3. Show them how to make a see-saw motion. One child slowly leans back, while the other child is pulled forward. Then the forward child leans back, pulling her partner forward. Encourage them to go slow and smoothly and not to jerk each other.

4. Encourage the children to row back and forth while singing "Row, Row, Row Your Boat."

Blowing Games

Children enjoy seeing the cause and effect of their breath.

ACTIVITY FOR AN INDIVIDUAL CHILD

Age group: 24–40 months
Duration of activity: 15 minutes

Table or accessible flat surface
Ping-Pong balls or cotton balls
Straws (optional)

1. Set your child in front of a table or an accessible flat surface.

2. Place cotton balls or Ping-Pong balls near the edge of the surface.

3. Demonstrate how to blow the items across the surface. The child may use a straw or blow directly.

For Children with Cognitive Disabilities

Cognitive disabilities are caused by impairment in intellectual processing and functioning; your child may be delayed in any number of areas. These activities will help her develop important problem-solving and critical thinking skills.

Mirror Mirror

Remember, all children learn through imitation. You can increase the complexity of your gestures and actions according to the child's ability.

ACTIVITY FOR AN INDIVIDUAL CHILD

Age group: 12–40 months
Duration of activity: 5 minutes

1. Place your child directly in front of you.

2. Encourage your child to mimic your facial expressions and motions.

3. Add complexity by having your child complete the motions with you simultaneously.

Your Turn, My Turn

This activity will help your child tune into you and learn reciprocity as well.

ACTIVITY FOR AN INDIVIDUAL CHILD

Age group: 24–40 months

Duration of activity: 10 minutes

A musical instrument (keyboard or drums work well)

1. Get your child's attention, say, "My turn," then play 1 or 2 notes or beats on the instrument.

2. Hand the instrument to your child and say, "Your turn," and prompt her to play as you did.

3. You may wish to expand this activity by asking the child to mimic what you are playing.

Find the Squeaker

Here is an activity that will help promote problem-solving skills.

ACTIVITY FOR AN INDIVIDUAL CHILD

Age group: 18–24 months

Duration of activity: 5 minutes

A small squeaky toy

When the child is not looking, hold the toy under or behind something and squeeze it.

For Children with Language Disabilities

Children learn language skills by using language. It is important that they have many opportunities to interact with others as they start to use language to communicate.

Microphone Craft

Bring out the star in your young child. Once he has a microphone,
put on some music and let him ham it up.

ACTIVITY FOR AN INDIVIDUAL CHILD

Age group: 18–40 months

Duration of activity: 10 minutes

Tin foil
Toilet paper tube
Black marker
Small craft foam ball

1. Help your child mold the tin foil over the paper tube so that both the bottom and sides are covered.

2. Have your child use the marker to color the craft ball.

3. Wedge the ball a third of the way into the tube.

Walking Finger Puppets

You can make an endless cast of puppet characters this way.

ACTIVITY FOR AN INDIVIDUAL CHILD

Age group: 18–40 months
Duration of activity: 15 minutes

Scissors
Cardboard or poster board
Crayons or markers

1. Discuss with your child what characters he would like to make.

2. Cut out an outline of the character 4" tall. The outline should include the head, neck, arms, and torso, but not the legs.

3. Cut 2 holes ¼" from the edge of the bottom of the torso. These holes should be wide enough for your child's fingers to fit through and approximately 1" apart.

4. Let your child decorate the puppet with crayons or markers.

5. Have your child stick his fingers through the holes. Show him how to use his fingers for the puppet's legs and move them to make the puppet walk.

Guessing Bag

This activity will encourage the child to use his sense of touch and to make inferences.

ACTIVITY FOR AN INDIVIDUAL CHILD OR A GROUP

Age group: 24–40 months
Duration of activity: 15 minutes

A variety of small household objects
Brown lunch bag

1. Place 3–6 objects in the bag. Be sure the objects do not have any sharp points or loose pieces.

2. Ask child to put his hand in the bag and feel one object at a time.

3. Encourage your child to describe what the object feels like and then guess what it is.

Sign Language

Learning sign language will help your toddler lessen frustration before she can communicate verbally. Even children without any disabilities can benefit from learning sign language.

ACTIVITY FOR AN INDIVIDUAL CHILD

Age group: 12–40 months
Duration of activity: 5 minutes

1. Sit near the child so that she is facing you and can see you clearly.

2. Demonstrate the sign while you say the word and act out or gesture the meaning.

3. Practice the signs with your child.

More: Close both hands together with thumb and middle finger touching and tap hands together.

Yes: Make a hand into a fist, holding it at about shoulder height and make fist bob back and forth.

No: Take index finger together with your middle finger and tap them together with your thumb.

Sleep: Fold hands palms together and place along cheek.

Happy: Take an extended hand and brush it in little circles up on the chest a couple of times.

Hungry: Take hand and make it into a c-shape with the palm facing the body. Start with a hand around your neck and move it down.

CHAPTER 14

Exploring Themes

When your child was an infant, his knowledge of the world around him was very limited. He only knew what was part of his daily, direct experience. Now, as he is growing, he is becoming more aware and more curious. He is meeting and interacting with more people and has the chance to explore beyond his own front door. Here are some ideas to help spark your child's interest as his experiences and knowledge expands.

Animal Activities

Many young children are fascinated by animals. Your child may enjoy watching videos of animals on television as well as seeing them at the zoo. Your child may begin her exploration of animals at home, with the family pet. Here are some activities for learning about more exotic animals.

Animal Safari

Engage your child's imagination as you take her on a pretend safari.
You may wish to add ambiance by playing a recording of jungle sounds in the background.

ACTIVITY FOR AN INDIVIDUAL CHILD

Age group: 18–40 months

Duration of activity: 10 minutes

Assorted stuffed animals

1. When your child is out of the room, hide a variety of stuffed animals.

2. Have your child return and search for the "wild" animals. Encourage her to name the animals that she finds.

Animal Reunion

Your toddler will learn more about animals as well as develop problem-solving skills with this activity.

ACTIVITY FOR AN INDIVIDUAL CHILD

Age group: 30–40 months

Duration of activity: 30 minutes

Pictures of animals
White craft glue
Index cards

1. Enlist your child's help in finding pictures of animals as adults and as babies. Old *National Geographic* magazines are a great source for animal pictures.

2. Glue one animal picture to each index card.

3. Have your child match up the babies with their parents.

Stuffed Snake

Here is a cute craft for your child. When she is done, she will have a new stuffed animal to play with.

ACTIVITY FOR AN INDIVIDUAL CHILD

Age group: 18–40 months

Duration of activity: 15 minutes

1 knee-high nylon stocking
Cotton fiber fill or wadded-up
    newspaper
Scissors
Felt pieces
White craft glue

1. Help your child stuff the stocking with the cotton or newspaper. Leave a few inches empty at the end, and tie a secure knot for the tail.

2. Cut out eyes and a mouth from the felt pieces. Let your child attach the features with glue. If your child is still putting things in her mouth, consider using a permanent marker to draw on facial features instead.

Monkey See, Monkey Do

Like toddlers, monkeys are known for their ability and desire to imitate. Here is a silly game that you can play with your child. This is basically a version of Follow the Leader. Consider reading the book Caps for Sale, by Esphyr Slobodkina, before you play this game.

ACTIVITY FOR AN INDIVIDUAL CHILD OR A GROUP

Age group: 18–40 months

Duration of activity: 10 minutes

The lead monkey performs different silly movements and dances that the other players must imitate. Take turns so everyone has a chance to be the lead monkey.

Dog Biscuits

Your child will have a blast making homemade treats for her dog.

ACTIVITY FOR AN INDIVIDUAL CHILD OR A GROUP

Age group: 18–40 months

Duration of activity: 45 minutes

½ cup cornmeal
6 tablespoons oil
⅔ cup water or meat broth
2 cups whole wheat flour
Cookie cutters

1. Stir all ingredients together. If dough seems a bit dry, add a few drops of water. If dough seems too wet, add more flour a little at a time.

2. Turn the dough out onto a floured surface. Show your child how to knead the dough.

3. Help her roll the dough out to ¼" thick. Let her cut out the biscuits with cookie cutters—a bone shape would be best.

4. Place biscuits on a cookie sheet and bake at 350°F for 30 minutes or until biscuits are light brown.

Hand-Print Sheep

Engage your child's senses with this personalized craft.

ACTIVITY FOR AN INDIVIDUAL CHILD OR A GROUP

Age group: 18–40 months

Duration of activity: 15 minutes

Construction paper
Pencil
White craft glue
Cotton balls
Crayons

1. Have your child put her hand palm down onto a piece of construction paper. Have her spread her fingers.

2. Use the pencil to trace around her hand. Turn the shape upside down; the four fingers become legs and the thumb is the head.

3. Show your child how to glue the cotton balls to create a fleecy effect.

4. Let her color in the feet and the face with crayons.

Community Helpers

At a very early age, children start to imitate adults. Your child may want to put on Mom's shoes or Dad's tie and pretend to be a grownup. He will start to show an interest in the roles that adults play. In addition to trying these activities with your child, consider making field trips to watch these community helpers in action.

Firefighters

This is a fun activity for a hot summer day. You can bet that when you combine water with a firefighter theme, you will have a hit on your hands.

ACTIVITY FOR AN INDIVIDUAL CHILD OR A GROUP

Age group: 18–40 months
Duration of activity: 30 minutes

Red, orange, and yellow sidewalk chalk
Garden hose
Small buckets (optional)

1. Enlist your child's help and use the chalk to draw a fire with lots of flames on the pavement.

2. Now the young firefighter needs to put out the fire! Help your child squirt the hose onto the drawing. As the chalk washes away, tell him he is dousing the flames.

3. If you have a group of children, you can use the buckets to set up a bucket brigade.

Special Delivery

Your child will enjoy using a variety of stickers and seals in the project. You may wish to let your child play with junk mail that you receive. Additionally, you may wish to let your child help you write and send a postcard to a family member or friend.

ACTIVITY FOR AN INDIVIDUAL CHILD

Age group: 18–40 months
Duration of activity: 10 minutes

Used stamps, postage seals, and
    address labels
Large envelope

1. You can show your child how to address and stamp an envelope, but let him explore freely with the materials.

2. If your child completes a postcard, walk him down to the corner mailbox and mail it!

Many Hats

Many professionals can be identified by the hats they wear. Here is a guessing game based on this concept. This activity suggests using pictures, but if you have real hats available, use those instead!

ACTIVITY FOR AN INDIVIDUAL CHILD

Age group: 30–40 months

Duration of activity: 15 minutes

White craft glue
Pictures of different hats
Index cards

Glue the pictures on the cards. Ask your child to look at each card and guess who wears that hat. (Suggested hats include a chef's hat, baseball cap, firefighter hat, police motorcycle helmet, nurse's cap, and hard hat.)

Transportation

Transportation is a fun theme to explore with your child. Because young children learn best through direct hands-on experience, take your child for a ride on different forms of transportation when you can. Perhaps your city still has a street car or trolley system. If you live in a rural area, can you go for a hayride on a local farm?

Rolling

Many forms of transportation move on wheels. Consider taking your child somewhere she can see the tracks that wheels leave in the mud or snow.

ACTIVITY FOR AN INDIVIDUAL CHILD

Age group: 18–40 months
Duration of activity: 15 minutes

Small toy cars and trucks
Dark-colored tempera paint
Shallow pie tin
Light-colored construction paper

1. Show your child how to gently dip the wheels of the vehicles into the paint, after you've poured it into the tin.

2. Let her create interesting patterns and designs by rolling the vehicles back and forth across the paper.

3. Be sure to wash the toys off when you are done.

My Car

Engage your child's imagination with the project. Remember your child can also build a boat, train, airplane, or whatever her imagination and creativity dictates.

ACTIVITY FOR AN INDIVIDUAL CHILD OR A GROUP

Age group: 18–40 months
Duration of activity: 30 minutes

Scissors
Large box (an appliance box works well)
Markers or tempera paint
Staple gun (optional)
Pie tins (optional)

1. Let your child decide where she would like you to cut windows or doors in the box.

2. Let your child decorate her vehicle however she wishes.

3. If you wish, you can staple on the pie tins for wheels.

Toy Airplane

Much simpler than a model, you and your toddler can construct this airplane.
Be aware that the plane will be too heavy and fragile to fly.

ACTIVITY FOR AN INDIVIDUAL CHILD

Age group: 18–40 months

Duration of activity: 20 minutes

Scissors
Paper towel tube
Poster board
Paper cup
Tissue paper scraps

1. Cut a 1" slit through both sides of the paper towel roll.

2. From the poster board, cut two wings. Make each the size and shape of an adult's index finger. Make sure that the wings will fit into the slots.

3. Cut tiny slits up from the rim of the paper cup. This is to slightly widen the top of the cup, which will become the cockpit.

4. Help your child slide the wings in the slits and place the cup over one opening of the tube. You may need to secure the cup with some glue.

5. Provide your child with tissue paper scraps to glue on for decoration.

The Wheels on the Bus

Do not be afraid to adapt this song to sing about other forms of transportation.
You can easily sing about the sails on the boat or the propeller on the plane.

ACTIVITY FOR AN INDIVIDUAL CHILD

Age group: 18–40 months

Duration of activity: 10 minutes

Sing or chant the following with your child. Encourage her to use appropriate motions:

The wheels on the bus go round and round,
Round and round, round and round.
The wheels on the bus go round and round,
All through the town.

(roll hands)

Other verses:

The wipers on the bus go swish, swish, swish.
The door on the bus goes open and shut.
The seats on the bus go bump, bump, bump.

Dinosaurs

Although the dinosaurs are long gone, they still capture the interest and imagination of young children. Many toddlers love to learn about these gigantic creatures from the past.

Digging for Bones

Here is a fun way to show your child how dinosaur fossils were found.
To extend this activity, let your child glue the bones together to create his own creature.
Here are two activities to help dinosaurs come alive again in your child's imagination.

ACTIVITY FOR AN INDIVIDUAL CHILD

Age group: 18–40 months

Duration of activity: 10 minutes

Smooth chicken bones
Sandbox

1. Start with smooth chicken bones. Be sure there are no sharp or splintered pieces.

2. Boil and thoroughly clean the bones. You may wish to add a drop of bleach to the boiling water to make them look older.

3. Bury the bones in the sandbox for your child to find.

Dinosaur Egg

Your child will be delighted to crack open the egg to find a dinosaur. Be sure to involve him in making the egg, too. You should closely supervise this activity. Because both the toy and the balloon can be choking hazards, this activity is best for children who no longer put things in their mouths.

ACTIVITY FOR AN INDIVIDUAL CHILD

Age group: 30–40 months

Duration of activity: 30 minutes plus 1 day for project to dry

1 balloon
Small plastic dinosaur toy
Papier Mâché
Tempera paint

1. Slightly inflate the balloon and insert the toy. Completely inflate the balloon and tie.

2. Coat the balloon with Papier Mâché (see Chapter 5)

3. Once the Papier Mâché is dry, your child can paint the egg.

The Ocean

There is a whole other world beneath the surface of the ocean. You do not have to live near the shore to introduce your child to this fascinating place under the sea. You can find some great props and artifacts such as shells and coral to share with your child.

Margarine Tub Jellyfish

You can create this cute little sea creature in a flash. If you want to have your child play with the jellyfish in the water, substitute yarn for the crepe-paper tentacles, and coat the tissue-paper-and-felt body with clear fingernail polish.

ACTIVITY FOR AN INDIVIDUAL CHILD

Age group: 18–40 months

Duration of activity: 15 minutes

White craft glue
Tissue paper
Margarine tub
Lengths of crepe paper, ribbon, or yarn
2 felt circles

1. Have your child glue tissue paper onto the margarine tub.

2. Once the body is dry, your child can glue on the crepe-paper tentacles and the felt eyes.

Deep-Sea Dive

This activity will engage your child's imagination and expand her vocabulary as she learns more about the ocean and aquatic life. For added excitement, let your child wear a snorkel mask.

ACTIVITY FOR AN INDIVIDUAL CHILD

Age group: 18–40 months

Duration of activity: 15 minutes

Blanket
Deep-sea items such as sea sponges, shells, starfish, toy sea animals, and pieces of coral

1. Drape a sheet or blanket over a table. Blue is best, but any color is okay.

2. Place a variety of deep-sea items under the table. Suggested items include sea sponges, shells, starfish, toy sea animals, and pieces of coral.

3. Have your child "dive" under the sheet (sea) and bring back a treasure. Ask her to identify what she found.

Paper Bag Whale

Your child may wish to make a group of these—if so, she can have a pod of whales.

ACTIVITY FOR AN INDIVIDUAL CHILD

Age group: 18–40 months

Duration of activity: 15 minutes

Brown paper bag
Newspaper
String
Gray and black paint

1. Have your child stuff the bag with crumpled up newspapers. Be sure that she leaves a little room near the opening.

2. Draw the bag closed and tie. Leave a little paper past the knot to serve as the tail.

3. Let your child paint her whale any way she wants.

Birds

Birds are everywhere. Take the binoculars outside and look for them. Bring some closer to your home for your child to observe. In your own backyard, you can set up a birdhouse, a birdbath, or a bird feeder to attract them.

Bird's Nest

If you have the chance, show your child a real-life bird's nest. Talk about what he would use to build a nest if he were a bird. When this nest is complete, your child might want to put a toy bird or eggs in it.

ACTIVITY FOR AN INDIVIDUAL CHILD

Age group: 18–40 months

Duration of activity: 20 minutes

Heavy-duty poster board
Mud
Leaves and grass
Sticks, twigs, and pine needles

1. With the poster board as a base, let your child make a mixture of the mud and the leaves and grass.

2. Help him form the mixture into a nest shape.

3. Let him add the sticks, twigs, and pine needles for interest.

Bird in the Cage

Your child will love finding the bird in the cage.
You might help your child make his own bird out of clay to use for this craft.
Remember to collect and dispose of broken balloon pieces, which can be a choking hazard.

ACTIVITY FOR AN INDIVIDUAL CHILD

Age group: 30–40 months

Duration of activity: 1 hour

Small toy bird, bought or homemade
Balloon
Water
White craft glue
Small bowl
Yarn or twine

1. Help your child insert the bird into the balloon.

2. Inflate and tie the balloon.

3. Mix the water and glue in a bowl to form a thick liquid.

4. Show your child how to dip pieces of yarn into the glue mixture. Have him let the excess glue drip off and then wrap the yarn around the balloon.

5. Encourage him to cover about 75 percent of the balloon.

6. When the glue is dry, pop the balloon. What will remain is the bird in the cage.

Way Up in the Sky

Your child will enjoy this cute action rhyme. It is more fun when you exaggerate the voices and use a high pitch when the birds are talking.

ACTIVITY FOR AN INDIVIDUAL CHILD

Age group: 18–40 months

Duration of activity: 15 minutes

Teach your child the following rhyme and the corresponding movements:

Way up in the sky
(raise arms in the air)

The little birds fly.
(flap arms)

While down in their nest,
The little birds rest.
(curl up arms like holding a baby)

With a wing on the left
(extend left arm)

And a wing on the right
(extend right arm)

The sweet little birdies sleep all through the night.
(press hands together on cheek)

Shhhhhhhhhhhhhhh!
(put finger to lips)

They're sleeping!
The bright sun comes up,
(raise arms in the air)

The dew falls away.
(pat in a downward motion)

"Good morning, good morning"
(wave and flap)

The little birds say!

Pond Life

Exploring pond life is a great way to learn more about nature and the environment. You can introduce your child to concepts of life cycles by observing frogs. You can begin a discussion about habitats, where different animals live and what they eat, too.

Lily-Pond Hop

Here is a cute way to teach your child a little bit about frogs and help develop her large motor skills as well. If your child is not yet coordinated enough to jump, help her leap or take a big step.

ACTIVITY FOR AN INDIVIDUAL CHILD

Age group: 18–40 months
Duration of activity: 15 minutes

Carpet squares or mats

1. Set up carpet squares or mats in a pattern around the room. Be sure that they are placed close enough together for your child to jump from one to another.

2. Talk about how frogs live in ponds and jump from lily pad to lily pad. Show your child how to jump like a frog.

I Had a Little Turtle

Promote the development of your child's fine motor skills with this cute rhyme.

ACTIVITY FOR AN INDIVIDUAL CHILD

Age group: 18–40 months
Duration of activity: 10 minutes

Teach your child the following rhyme and the corresponding motions:

I had a little turtle
(make fist)

Who lived in a box.
(draw outline of a square in the air)

He swam in the water
(swimming motion with arms)

And he climbed on the rocks.
(climbing motion with arms)

He snapped at a mosquito.
(clap fingers and thumb together on one hand)

He snapped at a flea.
(clap fingers and thumb together on one hand)

He snapped at a minnow
(clap fingers and thumb together on one hand)

And he snapped at me!
(clap fingers and thumb together on one hand)

He caught the mosquito,
(tap finger and thumb together and make chewing noises)

He caught the flea,
(tap finger and thumb together and make chewing noises)

He caught the minnow,
(tap finger and thumb together and make chewing noises)

But he couldn't catch me!
(shake finger back and forth)

Frog's Dinner

This fun game will help your child learn more about frogs while she develops coordination as well. You can get small plastic insects from a dollar store or a bait and tackle shop.

ACTIVITY FOR AN INDIVIDUAL CHILD

Age group: 18–40 months
Duration of activity: 15 minutes

White craft glue
Velcro discs
Small plastic flies and insects
Paper party blowers

1. Glue Velcro to each insect.

2. Attach Velcro to the end of the party blower.

3. Show your child how to blow the paper party favor so that it unrolls. Show her how to use this as a frog's tongue to catch the bugs.

Fairy Tales

Young children enjoy the classic fairy tales and rhymes. By sharing the stories and these activities, you will be helping your child develop literacy skills and imagination!

Sail Away

For a change, let your child drag a favorite toy or teddy bear around.

ACTIVITY FOR AN INDIVIDUAL CHILD

Age group: 18–36 months

Duration of activity: 10 minutes

Towel or blanket

1. Have your child sit or lay in the center of an old towel or blanket. If possible, do this on a hardwood or linoleum floor.

2. Slowly drag your child around and point out imaginary points of interest. Example: While passing the couch you can say, "Oh look, there goes the king's castle!"

Which Is the Best?

You may wish to start this activity by reading the story of Goldilocks and the Three Bears first.

ACTIVITY FOR AN INDIVIDUAL CHILD

Age group: 24–40 months

Duration of activity: 20 minutes

3 bowls of oatmeal with spoons (one very warm, one cold, and one just the way child likes it)

3 chairs or pillows (one with a board under it to make it stiff, one very soft, and one just the way the child likes it)

3 sweaters (one too small, one too big, and one just child's size)

1. Tell your child that not everyone is suited for the same things.

2. Present the oatmeal and call it porridge and ask your child to pick the one he would want.

3. Repeat with the cushions and the shirts. This time, let you child try them out if he wants.

Cinderella's Shoe

Bring the Cinderella story to life and promote problem-solving skills at the same time.

ACTIVITY FOR AN INDIVIDUAL CHILD

Age group: 24–36 months

Duration of activity: 10 minutes

1 fancy shoe or slipper

1. Read the story of Cinderella to your child.

2. Hide the chosen shoe and ask the child to find it.

3. You may choose to hide the shoe in a room or simply within a pile of other shoes.

Giant Shoes

What young child would pass up an activity that encourages him to be loud and rambunctious? Because your child won't be able to move as nimbly as usual, you need to closely supervise this activity.

ACTIVITY FOR AN INDIVIDUAL CHILD

Age group: 30–40 months

Duration of activity: 15 minutes

Scissors
2 shoeboxes
Masking tape
Recording of marching music

1. Cut a hole in the center of each shoebox lid just big enough to fit your child's foot.

2. Securely tape the lids to the boxes.

3. Help your child insert his feet into the boxes.

4. Once he is able to walk in his shoebox shoes, play some marching music and encourage him to march and stomp in time with the music.

CHAPTER 15

Exploring Concepts

Your young child learns best through play. This is her way of exploring and learning about her environment. For example, when your child is playing with LEGOS, she is learning about colors, counting, and spatial relationships. You can help promote your child's mastery of basic concepts with some of these fun, hands-on activities.

Shapes

When your child is learning about shapes, he is learning about basic mathematical and spatial concepts. Everything has a shape. Start to broaden your child's awareness by pointing out the shapes of everyday objects.

Shape Characters

These cute characters and rhymes will help your child with shape identification.

ACTIVITY FOR AN INDIVIDUAL CHILD

Age group: 18–40 months
Duration of activity: 15 minutes

Construction paper
Scissors
Crayons

1. From the construction paper, cut out a circle, a square, and a triangle.

2. Let your child color in facial features for each shape.

3. Teach your child the following rhymes for each shape:

   I am Suzy Circle, watch me bend
   Round and round from end to end.

   Tommy Triangle is the name for me;
   Count my sides: one, two, three.

   Sammy Square is my name;
   My four sides are all the same.

Shape Hunt

As your child searches for shapes, he is also developing visual discrimination skills that will help him with reading when he is older.

ACTIVITY FOR AN INDIVIDUAL CHILD

Age group: 18–40 months

Duration of activity: 15 minutes

Construction paper
Scissors

1. From the construction paper, cut out a circle, a square, and a triangle.

2. Work with one shape at a time. Show your child the shape, and tell him that he is going on a shape hunt. Help him find other items that are that shape. For example, show him the circle and then go around the room looking for circles. Help him find circles in things like a doorknob, a plate, or a clock.

Circle Prints

Let your child use his creativity while he explores the circle shape.

ACTIVITY FOR AN INDIVIDUAL CHILD

Age group: 18–40 months

Duration of activity: 20 minutes

Tempera paint
Pie tin
Circular objects
Construction paper

1. Pour some paint into the pie tin.

2. Have your child help you find circular items to use. Some suggested items include jar lids or the rim of a paper cup.

3. Show your child how to dip items in the paint and then press them onto the paper to create circle prints.

Shape Animals

This activity will help your child use problem-solving skills as well as help him with shape identification.

1. Precut a variety of shapes from the construction paper, making multiples of each shape as well as different sizes of each.

2. Show your toddler how to arrange the shapes to create the forms of animals. For example, a triangle could be the head, and four circles can be used for paws. Glue each animal to the poster board.

3. Help your child identify the shapes that he uses. Encourage your child to label the animal that he made. Did he make a lion, a bear, or perhaps a new species altogether?

Colors

There are many activities that can help your child learn color identification. The most successful activities are hands-on and engage your child's senses. Here are just a few to get you started.

Rainbow Discs

Here is a way for your child to see the world through many-colored lenses.
This activity can also serve as an introductory lesson on mixing colors.

ACTIVITY FOR AN INDIVIDUAL CHILD

Age group: 18–40 months
Duration of activity: 20 minutes

6 paper plates
Scissors
Red, yellow, and blue cellophane
White craft glue

1. Put two paper plates together and cut a hole in the center about the size of a plum.

2. Cut a piece of colored cellophane slightly larger than the hole.

3. Glue the cellophane to the top of one plate to cover the hole.

4. Set the second plate on top of the first and help your child glue them together. Now you have a rainbow disc for your child to look through.

5. Repeat these steps to make two more discs in the remaining colors. Show your child how to overlap the discs to create new colors.

Color Lotto

Lotto games enhance your child's memory and problem-solving skills.
You can adapt this game for shape, letter, or number recognition as well.

ACTIVITY FOR AN INDIVIDUAL CHILD

Age group: 30–40 months
Duration of activity: 30 minutes

Scissors
Index cards
Colored construction paper
White craft glue

1. Make two lotto cards for each color by cutting an index card in half crosswise.

2. Cut pieces of colored construction paper to fit the halves of each card.

3. Have your child help glue the paper on the cards. Each card should have a colored side and a blank side.

4. Mix the cards and arrange them in rows colored side down.

5. Your child is to flip over two cards and try to find a match. When she does, she can remove the cards. If she does not make a match, she is to turn the cards back over and try again. Do not worry about strictly following the rules. Your child may need to turn over more than two cards or even keep them facing up.

Fishing for Colors

This fun game will help your child develop her eye-hand coordination while learning to identify colors. You need to closely supervise this activity at all times—the "fishing line" could wrap around your child, and the magnets and clips could pose a choking hazard.

ACTIVITY FOR AN INDIVIDUAL CHILD

Age group: 30–40 months

Duration of activity: 20 minutes

1 piece of string 2' long
1 smooth stick or dowel rod
1 small magnet
Scissors
Colored construction paper
Paper clips

1. Tie the string around the end of the stick and then attach the magnet to serve as the hook.

2. Cut the construction paper into fish shapes several inches in length.

3. Attach a paper clip to the head of each fish.

4. You can place the fish on the floor or put them in an empty aquarium.

5. Show your child how to use the magnetized fishing pole to "catch" a fish. Have her identify the color of the fish she catches.

Squish and Mix

This is a great sensory activity that will help your child observe what happens when colors are mixed. Be sure to talk to your child about what she sees.

ACTIVITY FOR AN INDIVIDUAL CHILD

Age group: 18–40 months

Duration of activity: 15 minutes

Tempera paint
Zip-top bags

1. Add a small amount of the blue and red paints in a zip-top bag and seal. Place that bag inside a second bag and seal.

2. Let your child squish and knead the bag to mix the paints and create the color purple.

3. Repeat with other color combinations (such as blue and yellow to make green, white and red to make pink, etc.).

Numbers

Children develop a mathematical awareness at an early age. Although your toddler is not ready for mathematical equations, you can start to introduce him to the concepts of quantity and the symbolic representation of quantity.

Count Through the Day

You do not need to plan a formal activity to help your child develop number and counting concepts.

ACTIVITY FOR AN INDIVIDUAL CHILD

Age group: 30–40 months

As you go through the day with your child, count with him. Point out things in his environment and encourage him to count with you. "Let's count how many cookies are on the plate." "Look, Andy, there are a lot of birds on the tree, let's count them!"

Three Little Kittens

Use this popular rhyme to reinforce number concepts with your toddler.
You can also do this activity with The Three Bears and their bowls of porridge.

ACTIVITY FOR AN INDIVIDUAL CHILD

Age group: 30–40 months

Duration of activity: 10 minutes

3 photos of different cats
6 mittens (or paper cutouts of mittens)

1. Recite the following rhyme for your toddler:

    Three little kittens,
    They lost their mittens,
    And they began to cry,
    Oh, mother dear,
    We sadly fear
    Our mittens we have lost.
    What! Lost your mittens,
    You naughty kittens!
    Then you shall have no pie.
    Mee-ow, mee-ow, mee-ow, mee-ow.
    You shall have no pie.

    The three little kittens,
    They found their mittens,
    And they began to cry,
    Oh, mother dear,
    See here, see here,
    Our mittens we have found.
    What! Found your mittens,
    You darling kittens!
    Then you shall have some pie.
    Mee-ow, mee-ow, mee-ow, mee-ow.
    You shall have some pie.

2. Set up the three pictures and have your child count and distribute the mittens for each cat.

Birthday Cake

Here is a fun way to help your child see the relationship between numerals and quantity.

ACTIVITY FOR AN INDIVIDUAL CHILD

Age group: 30–40 months

Duration of activity: 15 minutes

Scissors
Construction paper
Markers
White craft glue

1. Cut the construction paper in the shape of a cake. Repeat to make 5 cakes.

2. Mark the assigned number on the side of the cake.

3. Cut out 15 thin rectangle shapes for candles. Cut out tiny yellow teardrop shapes for flames and glue them onto the candles.

4. For each cake, help your child identify the number and glue on the appropriate number of candles.

Number Bag

Here is a fun outdoor activity that will reinforce number concepts and counting skills.

ACTIVITY FOR AN INDIVIDUAL CHILD

Age group: 30–40 months

Duration of activity: 10 minutes

Marker
Small brown-paper lunch bags

1. Mark each bag with a number, starting simply with just 1, 2, and 3.

2. Take your child outdoors where he can find things to collect, such as leaves or stones. Direct him to put the appropriate number of items in each bag.

Letters

Your young child is just starting to learn to decode and interpret symbols. Although you may consider letter recognition an important skill, be sure to keep the learning activities fun! Letter recognition is only one step in developing literacy skills and will not be fully mastered for a few years yet. (You will find more literacy activities in Chapter 11.)

ABC Dominoes

Help your child with letter recognition and problem solving with this twist on a classic game.

ACTIVITY FOR AN INDIVIDUAL CHILD

Age group: 30–40 months

Duration of activity: 15 minutes

Index cards
Markers

1. On each index card, draw a line crosswise down the center.

2. On each side of the line, print a letter of the alphabet so that the top of each letter faces the line in the middle. To keep it simple, you may wish to use only a few letters.

3. Show your child how to match up the ends as you would with regular dominoes.

There's a "B" in My Soup

Help your child with letter recognition and awareness. Show her how there are letters all around her.

ACTIVITY FOR AN INDIVIDUAL CHILD

Age group: 30–40 months
Duration of activity: 15 minutes

1. Have your child pick out and identify letters in her alphabet soup or cereal.

2. For a variation, give your child some dry alphabet cereal or noodles and challenge her to find certain letters. Perhaps you can help her spell her name.

Letter Collages

Here is a concrete way to help your toddler with letter identification and the sounds the letters make. Close supervision is needed when you are working with small objects.

ACTIVITY FOR AN INDIVIDUAL CHILD

Age group: 30–40 months
Duration of activity: 30 minutes

Scissors
Poster board
White craft glue
Variety of small objects

1. Cut your chosen letters from the poster board. Make them 8"–10" high, leaving plenty of room to glue objects.

2. Help your child select and then glue appropriate objects onto the letter. For example, glue buttons on the "B" or glue pennies on the "P."

Time

Time is one of the more complex concepts you can't expect your young child to comprehend. This is because your child cannot see or touch time. Time is an abstract concept, so any meaningful activities must be hands-on and relevant for your child.

How Long?

Although your child is not ready to measure time with a clock,
you can introduce him to the basic concept of time passage in a concrete way.

ACTIVITY FOR AN INDIVIDUAL CHILD

Age group: 30–40 months
Duration of activity: Variable

Challenge your child to guess/estimate how long certain activities will take to complete. You can use an hourglass, a timer, or simply count. Sample activities to time include brushing his teeth, walking up the steps, or singing his favorite song.

What Comes Next?

The progression of time follows a predictable rhythm.
This activity will help your child track the passage of time as he learns to predict and anticipate events.

ACTIVITY FOR AN INDIVIDUAL CHILD

Age group: 30–40 months

Duration of activity: 15 minutes

5 or 6 index cards
White craft glue
Magazine pictures depicting routine
 activities

1. On each index card, glue a picture depicting a child performing a routine activity. Examples might be a child getting dressed, taking a bath, eating dinner, or listening to a bedtime story.

2. Help your toddler to put the cards in order as they occur in his day. Be sure to discuss the concepts of routine and sequence with him: "What do you do after you come home from Grandma's house?" or "Do you take a bath after dinner time or before dinner time?"

Spatial Concepts

Helping your child learn spatial concepts will help her master mathematical and reading skills when she enters school. These activities will also help her to learn to follow directions and build her vocabulary.

In and Out the Doors

By playing this fun game, your child will be learning the directions in, out, and through. It is also a great way to build large motor skills. Once your child has mastered the basic activity, add excitement by challenging her to do it faster and faster.

ACTIVITY FOR A GROUP

Age group: 30–40 months
Duration of activity: Variable

1. Participants hold hands while standing in a circle. Players need to stand far enough apart that they can hold their arms outstretched.

2. Players can make one of two configurations. If they hold their arms straight out, they are making a window. If they raise their arms, they are creating a door.

3. One player stands in the center. She then goes in and out of the circle by passing through the doors the other players have made. She cannot go through any windows. Players in the circle can change from a door to a window as they choose.

Hey Diddle Diddle

Use the famous nursery rhyme to help your child learn spatial concepts.

ACTIVITY FOR A GROUP

Age group: 30–40 months
Duration of activity: 15 minutes

Masking tape
Cut-out or photograph of the moon
1 sheet poster board
Cut-out or photograph of a cow

1. Tape the moon onto the poster board. Stick a loop of tape to the back of the cow.

2. Teach your child the classic nursery rhyme "Hey Diddle Diddle." Ask your child questions like, "Did you ever see a cow jump over the moon?" or "Do you think a cow can really jump that high?"

3. Ask your child to stick the cow "over" the moon.

4. Introduce variations to the rhyme and have your child place the cow in the appropriate place each time. Examples: the cow hid under the moon, the cow danced beside the moon, and so on.

The Noble Duke of York

This is a traditional action song that will get your child moving while she learns directions.

Teach your child the following song and the movements that accompany it:

The Noble Duke of York,
He had 10,000 men
(hold up ten fingers)

He marched them all straight up a hill
(point up and rise up on tiptoes)

And marched them down again
(point down and squat to the ground)

And when they're up, they're up up up!
(point up and rise up on tiptoes)

And when they're down, they're down, down, down!
(point down and squat to the ground)

And when they're only halfway up,
(stoop halfway)

They're neither
Up nor down!
(quickly jump up and then land on the ground)

Hurrah for Hula Hoops

Your child may be too young to swivel a hoop around her hips, but she can still have fun while she is learning.

ACTIVITY FOR A GROUP

Age group: 30–40 months
Duration of activity: 15 minutes

Give your child directions for moving with the hula hoop. Here are just a few ideas to get you started.

With the hoop on the ground:

- Stand inside the hoop.
- Jump out of the hoop.
- Walk around the hoop.

While holding the hoop:

- Put the hoop over your head.
- Step through the hoop.

CHAPTER 16

Seasonal Activities

Your child still has a lot to learn about the world around him. Help your child observe the natural changes that occur with the seasons. He will be learning about the predictable rhythms of time. Because the most concrete signs of the seasons are changes in nature, you will find that the activities in this chapter often use materials found outside.

Harvest-Time Fun

Harvest time is a fun season to celebrate with your child. Take this opportunity to talk about where food comes from. If you can, consider a trip to a local commercial farm. Many have programs for children where they can pick their own pumpkins, taste fresh apple cider, or participate in other activities.

Apple Prints

Celebrate harvest time with a bounty of fresh apples.
This activity will help your child have fun with this popular fruit.

ACTIVITY FOR AN INDIVIDUAL CHILD

Age group: 18–40 months
Duration of activity: 10 minutes

Knife
1 apple
Paper towel
Tempera paint
Shallow pie tin
Light-colored construction paper

1. Cut the apple in half crosswise. Dry off the inside with a paper towel.

2. Pour a small amount of paint into the pie tin.

3. Show your toddler how to grasp the apple to dip it into the paint. Have her press the painted apple on the paper to create a print. The effect will look a little like a star.

Cornucopia

*What is a more popular symbol of harvest than the cornucopia (horn of plenty)?
Here is an easy way to make one. While you are working on this project,
take the time to discuss with your child where different foods come from.*

ACTIVITY FOR AN INDIVIDUAL CHILD

Age group: 30–40 months

Duration of activity: 20 minutes

1 sheet brown construction paper
Masking tape
Magazines
Scissors

1. Roll the sheet of brown paper to create a horn shape. Secure the edges with tape.

2. Go through the magazines with your child to find appropriate items to add to the cornucopia. Explain that the cornucopia holds foods from a harvest: fruits and vegetables that have been picked.

3. Assist your child in cutting out the magazine pictures or have her tear out the pictures. Let her tape the food into the cornucopia.

Corn Rolling

*This simple painting activity produces a unique effect. You may also wish to have your toddler try
painting and printing with other vegetables, such as potatoes, cauliflower, and green peppers.*

ACTIVITY FOR AN INDIVIDUAL CHILD

Age group: 18–40 months

Duration of activity: 15 minutes

1 dried ear of corn
Tempera paint
Shallow pie tin
Light-colored construction paper

1. Have your child roll the corncob in the paint in the tin the same way that you would a paint roller.

2. Your child can then roll out different patterns and designs on the paper.

Harvest Bowling

Help develop your child's motor skills while exposing her to some fall vegetables. Your child will enjoy exploring the different colors and interesting textures. Look for gourds that are shaped like bottles, with a wide base and thin neck.

ACTIVITY FOR AN INDIVIDUAL CHILD OR A GROUP

Age group: 30–40 months

Duration of activity: 20 minutes

5 small dried gourds
Masking tape
1 or 2 small round pumpkins

1. Set the gourds up like bowling pins.

2. Stick a strip of masking tape to the floor to make a start line. This should be quite close to the gourds, as the pumpkins will not roll very far.

3. Show your child how to roll the pumpkins to knock down the gourds. Don't worry about keeping score.

Leaves Are Changing

If you are fortunate to live somewhere where the leaves change colors in the fall, be sure to try some of these activities. When you do activities around fall leaves, you are promoting your child's observation skills. This is a wonderful way for your child to see how things change and to observe the passage of time and seasons.

Leaf Rubbings

This is a great way for your child to explore the different shapes and textures of autumn leaves. Avoid leaves that are already dried out. This simple project seems to work like magic.

ACTIVITY FOR AN INDIVIDUAL CHILD

Age group: 30–40 months

Duration of activity: 10 minutes

A variety of autumn leaves that your child has collected

Light-colored bond paper

Peeled crayons

1. Have your child place one leaf or a group of leaves under the sheet of paper.

2. Show your child how to use the side of a crayon to rub on the paper. The shape and texture of the leaf will be revealed.

Leaf Crown

Your child will enjoy making this crown. He can use it as a prop in his imaginative play.

ACTIVITY FOR AN INDIVIDUAL CHILD

Age group: 18–40 months

Duration of activity: 10 minutes

Measuring tape

Scissors

2 sheets construction paper

Stapler

White craft glue

A variety of autumn leaves

1. Measure the circumference of your child's head. Cut 2"-wide strips from the construction paper and staple them together to make a band that will fit your child's head.

2. Help your child glue the leaves to his crown.

Leaf Glitter

Here is a new way to add pizzazz to your child's drawing and artwork.
You may choose to add store-bought glitter to the mix.

ACTIVITY FOR AN INDIVIDUAL CHILD OR A GROUP

Age group: 18–40 months

Duration of activity: 20 minutes

Colorful autumn leaves, slightly dry
White craft glue
Construction paper

1. Help the child crumble up the leaves into fine pieces.

2. Let your child sprinkle leaf "glitter" to his glue design on the paper. He may also choose to add the leaf glitter to other pictures he has made.

Scary Things

You may or may not choose to celebrate Halloween with your young child. Toddlers have a great deal of difficulty understanding the difference between fact and fantasy, so common symbols and sights of this holiday can be truly frightening for them. Giving your child hands-on, safe opportunities to explore scary things can help her understand and feel more in control.

Egg-Carton Bat

Popular culture has done much to malign the reputation of bats. Most bats are harmless and even helpful in keeping the insect population in check. You can talk to your child about bats while you do this craft.

ACTIVITY FOR AN INDIVIDUAL CHILD

Age group: 30–40 months

Duration of activity: 15 minutes

Scissors
1 cardboard egg carton
Black tempera paint
Red tempera paint
Small paintbrushes
Black construction paper
White craft glue

1. Cut off one cup of the egg carton. This will be the bat's body.

2. Let your child paint the cup black and then use the red paint to add facial features.

3. While the paint is drying, cut out two wings from the construction paper. Each wing should be no longer than 2" long.

4. Show your child how to glue the wings onto the bat.

Tissue Paper Ghosts

This is such a simple activity with a very cute result.
Your child may want to make a lot of ghosts and then hang them around the house for decoration.

ACTIVITY FOR AN INDIVIDUAL CHILD

Age group: 30–40 months

Duration of activity: 10 minutes

Tissue paper such as Kleenex
Cotton balls
Masking tape
Yarn cut into 12" sections
Fine-tip black marker

1. Show your child how to drape the sheet of tissue paper over the cotton ball.

2. Help your child secure the cotton ball by wrapping a piece of masking tape tightly below. This will form the neck. If you wish to hang the ghost later, stick a piece of yarn under the tape.

3. Your child can use the marker to draw on the eyes and mouth. Hang the ghost where the breeze will catch it and make it fly.

Paper Plate Spiders

Even if your child is afraid of spiders, she is still likely to enjoy this cute craft.

ACTIVITY FOR AN INDIVIDUAL CHILD

Age group: 30–40 months

Duration of activity: 15 minutes

Crayons
2 paper plates
Hole punch
2' of yarn
White craft glue
8 strips black construction paper

1. Let your child color the front of the plates. She can draw in a face for the spider if she wishes.

2. Punch a hole in the center of one of the plates. Knot the end and thread the yarn through the hole from front to back. This will be used to hang the spider.

3. Help your child glue the black strips onto the back of one plate. These are the spider's legs—they should be evenly spaced and should stick out past the rim of the plate.

4. Glue the two plates together back to back to complete the spider.

Masks

Masks can be particularly frightening for a young child, who may not recognize the transformed face as someone she knows and may not understand that the transformation is temporary. This activity may help your child overcome any fear, but if she is reluctant to wear the mask, don't force her.

ACTIVITY FOR AN INDIVIDUAL CHILD

Age group: 18–40 months

Duration of activity: 15 minutes

Scissors
Paper plate
Crayons and markers
White craft glue
Craft stick
Mirror

1. Cut wide holes in the paper plate to make eyes and a mouth.

2. Have your child decorate the back of the plate to create a face.

3. Glue the craft stick onto the bottom to serve as a handle. Your child can then hold up the mask to her face. Let her see herself in a mirror.

Spider Webs

Your toddler will enjoy making this unusual craft.

1. Pour some glue into the shallow bowl.

2. Show your child how to dip each noodle individually into the glue. Have her hold the noodle over the bowl to let any excess glue drip off.

3. Let her arrange the noodles onto the waxed paper in her version of a cobweb design.

4. When the design is dry, you can lift it off the paper and hang it from the ceiling.

Let It Snow!

When you wake up to find that it has snowed overnight, you may be annoyed or even angry. To you, snow means shoveling, hazardous roads, and longer commutes. To your child, however, snow is a magical wonderland! Take the time to remember the fun of playing in the snow.

Jack Frost

Your child can paint the windows with this mixture to make it look like Jack Frost has just paid a visit. When you wish, you can clean the window off with a wet cloth. Supervise your child closely so that he does not ingest any of the mixture.

ACTIVITY FOR AN INDIVIDUAL CHILD

Age group: 18–40 months
Duration of activity: 45 minutes

5 tablespoons Epsom salts
1 cup beer
Sponge
Facial tissue or paper towels

1. Dissolve the Epsom salts in the beer. It should foam. Let this sit for ½ hour before using.

2. While you are waiting, clean off a window that your toddler can easily reach.

3. Your child can dip the sponge into the mixture and swirl it onto the window.

4. Pat the designs gently with wet tissues or paper towels.

5. When the painting dries, the salt crystals will sparkle, giving the window a frosted appearance.

Snowy Picture

Here is a special way to create a seasonal picture.
Perhaps you and your child can think of other ways to create a snowy effect.

ACTIVITY FOR AN INDIVIDUAL CHILD

Age group: 30–40 months
Duration of activity: 15 minutes

White tempera paint
Shallow pie tin
Small paper doilies
Dark-colored construction paper
Old toothbrush

1. Pour the paint into the pie tin.

2. Have your child arrange the doilies on the paper and paint over them to create snowflake patterns. Remove and discard the doilies.

3. Let your child dip the bristles of the toothbrush into the paint. Show him how to flick the bristles over the paper to splatter the paint for a snowy effect. Be sure he holds the brush far from his eyes.

Ice-Cube Painting

This is a fun craft and science activity all in one.
If you don't have the paint, you can also use Kool-Aid or Jell-O powder.

ACTIVITY FOR AN INDIVIDUAL CHILD OR A GROUP

Age group: 18–40 months

Duration of activity: 15 minutes

Ice cube tray
Craft sticks or small tongue depressors
Powdered tempera paint
Construction paper or poster board

1. Make a tray of ice cubes. Freeze each cube with a craft stick sticking in so that you have a square Popsicle.

2. Let your child sprinkle the powdered paint on the paper.

3. Show your child how to use the ice cube on a stick as a paintbrush. The colors will swirl as the ice melts.

Snow Castle

Tired of snowmen? Why not pretend you're at the beach? Your child can even paint the completed castles by spraying them with a mixture of water and tempera paint or food coloring.

ACTIVITY FOR AN INDIVIDUAL CHILD

Age group: 18–40 months

Duration of activity: 20 minutes

Sand pails
Small shovels and spoons
A snowy day

Show your child how to fill the bucket with snow. Have him dump and mold a castle from snow.

Rainbow Melt

Your child will enjoy watching the colors run as he learns a little bit about science, too.

ACTIVITY FOR AN INDIVIDUAL CHILD

Age group: 18–40 months

Duration of activity: 25 minutes

Salt
Food coloring in various colors
Paper cups
Ice (cubes or large block)
Shallow pie tin

1. Mix 1 tablespoon of salt with a few drops of food coloring and put into a paper cup. Repeat process for different colors.

2. Place the ice in the pie tin.

3. Let your child sprinkle the colored salt liquid over the ice. Discuss what happens. Encourage him to observe how the colors run when the ice melts.

Arctic Animals and Hibernation

Young children are usually fascinated by animals. When you talk to your child about hibernation, share information about the habits of animals but also about the basic needs of both animals and people. How do we stay warm in the winter? Do we need to rest?

Groundhog Puppet

Here's a cute puppet variation. Your child may want to create an entire story around the groundhog that she creates.

ACTIVITY FOR AN INDIVIDUAL CHILD

Age group: 30–40 months

Duration of activity: 10 minutes

1 small paper cup
Tempera paint
Scissors
1 piece of brown felt
Fine-tip black marker
White craft glue
1 craft stick

1. Have your child decorate a paper cup for the burrow. When the paint is dry, poke a hole in the bottom of the cup.

2. Cut a quarter-sized circle from the felt to make a head for the puppet. Your child can draw the face on with the marker.

3. Help your child glue the groundhog head onto the craft stick. Turn the cup upside down and push the bottom of the stick into the hole you made in the cup. Your child can push the stick up from the inside of the cup to make the groundhog pop up.

Find Me in the Snow

This activity will help your child develop the visual discriminatory skills she needs for reading. Be sure to use this opportunity to talk about camouflage and how it can protect an animal. You can use either magazine clippings or make your own animal outline shapes from white bond paper.

ACTIVITY FOR AN INDIVIDUAL CHILD

Age group: 18–40 months

Duration of activity: 10 minutes

Scissors
White bond paper
White craft glue
1 sheet white poster board

1. Cut the shapes of a number of white animals (polar bear, lemming, snow hare) from the paper and glue to the poster board.

2. Challenge your child to find the animals hiding in the snow.

Penguin Walk

This is fun way to learn a little about penguins and help your child develop large motor skills at the same time.

ACTIVITY FOR AN INDIVIDUAL CHILD

Age group: 30–40 months

Duration of activity: 10 minutes

Small beach ball

1. Help your child place the beach ball between her knees. Challenge her to keep the ball there while walking across the room. Once she masters this, have her hold her arms out to completely imitate a penguin.

2. Teach her the following song to go along with the walk. It is sung to the tune of "I'm a Little Teapot":

   I'm a little penguin, oh so bold.
   I live where it's very cold.
   I can waddle fast and walk on ice.
   I think cold is very nice.

Hibernation Party

Here is a fun and concrete way to teach your child about hibernation.

ACTIVITY FOR AN INDIVIDUAL CHILD OR A GROUP

Age group: 30–40 months

Duration of activity: 30 minutes

Snack food
Blankets and pillows

1. Explain to your child that today you are going to pretend to be bears and hibernate.

2. In order to have energy, you need to eat well before hibernating. Serve the child a nice snack.

3. Have your child help you set up a cozy bear den. You can do this by draping a blanket over a table. Use extra pillows and blankets to make the den comfortable.

4. Turn out the lights and encourage your child to curl up inside the den and pretend to sleep.

5. After a short time, turn on the lights and announce that spring is here! When bears emerge from their den, they do a lot of stretching. They may even be a bit hungry again!

Springtime

Springtime is a time of change. Consider taking your toddler for a walk to observe the first signs of spring. Look for budding trees, birds returning from the south, the first signs of early flowers such as crocuses, and more.

Wind Sock

When your child is done with this project, be sure to hang it somewhere it can catch the wind. Do not be surprised if your child wants to make more than one.

ACTIVITY FOR AN INDIVIDUAL CHILD

Age group: 18–40 months

Duration of activity: 20 minutes

Crayons or markers
1 large sheet poster board
Masking tape
Hole punch
Yarn or twine
Crepe or tissue paper

1. Have your child use crayons or markers to decorate both sides of the poster board.

2. Roll the board into a cylinder and tape it securely on the edges.

3. Punch a hole at one end and attach a yarn loop for hanging.

4. Let your toddler tape strips of the crepe or tissue paper to the other end.

Blossom Trees

Although they will not smell as nice as real flowering trees, you will be surprised how realistic these trees look. If you don't want to use popcorn, you can have your child make little blossoms by crumpling up small pieces of tissue paper or Kleenex.

ACTIVITY FOR AN INDIVIDUAL CHILD OR A GROUP

Age group: 18–40 months

Duration of activity: 15 minutes

Brown crayon
Light-colored construction paper
White craft glue
1 cup popped popcorn

1. Have your child use the crayon to draw a tree trunk and branches on the paper.

2. Show your child how to glue the popcorn on the branches to make the blossoms. It works best if he puts a dab of glue on the paper rather than on the popcorn kernel.

Soufflé Flowers

This simple activity results in a craft with a nice fragrance that lasts a long time. Perhaps your child will want to make a whole bouquet.

ACTIVITY FOR AN INDIVIDUAL CHILD OR A GROUP

Age group: 30–40 months

Duration of activity: 15 minutes

Paper baking cups or mini soufflé cups
Watercolor paints
Paintbrush
Perfume
Cotton ball
White craft glue
Pipe cleaner

1. Show your toddler how to open and spread the baking cups out.

2. Let your toddler paint the cups.

3. Help your child dab a small amount of perfume onto the cotton ball. When the paint is dry, he can glue the ball into the center of the flower.

4. Help your child attach the pipe cleaner to make a stem for the flower.

Egg-Carton Tulips

This creative craft can be used for a festive centerpiece.

ACTIVITY FOR AN INDIVIDUAL CHILD OR A GROUP

Age group: 30–40 months

Duration of activity: 25 minutes

Scissors
Egg carton (cardboard works better than Styrofoam)
Paintbrush
Tempera paint
Pipe cleaners or chenille sticks

1. Cut the carton into individual egg cups.

2. Let your toddler paint the cups.

3. When the paint is dry, use the scissors to poke a small hole in the bottom of the cups.

4. Thread a pipe cleaner through each one. Pull enough of each into the center to twist a small loop. This will keep it secure as a stem and create a little stamen. Always be sure that there are no sharp wires on the ends of the pipe cleaners.

Summer Activities

Here are a few activities to celebrate summertime. Remember that the most valuable way for your toddler to learn about summertime is through experience. Take the time to watch clouds roll by, go for a walk in a meadow, or drink homemade lemonade under the shade of a big tree.

Sunflowers

This cheery craft will brighten up any summer day.
Children seem drawn to these giants of the flower world.

ACTIVITY FOR AN INDIVIDUAL CHILD OR A GROUP

Age group: 18–40 months

Duration of activity: 15 minutes

Marker
Brown, yellow, and green construction paper
Scissors
White craft glue
Sunflower seeds

1. Draw a circle on the brown paper and the outline of eight yellow triangles on the yellow paper. Make the circle as big or small as you want the sunflower to be. Size the triangles so that side by side, they will go all the way around the circle. Cut a stem from the green paper.

2. Either cut the shapes out yourself, or assist your child in doing so.

3. Show your child how to glue the pieces together to create a flower. When the flower is dry, she can glue on the sunflower seeds in the middle.

Sun on a Stick

This project makes a cute decoration to place into a potted plant.
It can also be used as a puppet or a hand-held fan.

ACTIVITY FOR AN INDIVIDUAL CHILD

Age group: 18–40 months

Duration of activity: 15 minutes

Scissors
2 paper plates
Yellow and orange tempera paint or crayons
White craft glue
Craft stick

1. Cut a big circle from the center of one paper plate.

2. Have your child paint or color the circle orange. Have her paint or color the intact plate yellow.

3. Help your child glue the orange circle onto the yellow plate.

4. Glue the craft stick onto the bottom to serve as a handle.

Everlasting Sand Castle

Bring the beach home with this unique craft activity.

ACTIVITY FOR AN INDIVIDUAL CHILD

Age group: 18–40 months

Duration of activity: 20 minutes

4 cups sand
2 cups cornstarch
1 tablespoon plus 1 teaspoon cream of
  tartar
3 cups hot water

1. Mix all ingredients together and let cool.

2. Your child can use the mixture to build a castle by hand, or she can use shallow plastic containers for molds. Coat the containers with Vaseline before using.

3. Give the castle three days to dry.

Flowery Window Clings

Decorate any sunny window with this easy project.

ACTIVITY FOR AN INDIVIDUAL CHILD

Age group: 18–40 months

Duration of activity: 15 minutes

Scissors
Clear contact paper
Flower blossoms and leaves

1. Cut 4" squares of clear contact paper.

2. Help your child place flower blossoms and leaves on the sticky side of the paper. Leave enough of the contact paper uncovered that it will stick to the window.

3. Carefully pick up the squares and press on the window.

4. When you choose to take the flowers off the window, you can remove the excess adhesive with nail-polish remover.

CHAPTER 17

Holiday Activities

Holidays are special times when ordinary routines are broken and there are new foods, visitors, and activities. The excitement can be overwhelming for young children. Although you want a holiday to be fun for your young child, remember that he may need some quiet one-on-one time with you. Take some time out of your hectic schedule to try one of these activities with him.

New Year's Day

Your young child will probably be fast asleep long before the clock strikes midnight. But she can still participate in some of the festivities. This is a great time to talk to her about the passage of time.

New Year's Noisemakers

*Your child will enjoy making noise and helping to celebrate the new year
without having to stay up until midnight.*

ACTIVITY FOR AN INDIVIDUAL CHILD

Age group: 18–40 months

Duration of activity: 10 minutes

Pencil
Toilet paper tube
Scissors
Waxed paper
Masking tape
Crayons

1. Use the pencil to poke three holes on one side of the tube. Make holes in a straight line and leave at least 1" between them.

2. Cut a square of waxed paper large enough to cover the opening of the tube. Help your child secure the waxed paper over the end of the tube nearest the hole with a long piece of masking tape.

3. Let your child decorate the horn with crayons. Show her how to blow into the horn to make noise.

New Year's Party Hat

You can adapt this basic craft and let your child make a hat for any special occasion.

ACTIVITY FOR AN INDIVIDUAL CHILD

Age group: 18–40 months

Duration of activity: 15 minutes

2 sheets construction paper in bright colors
Stapler
Crayons
Scissors
Glitter
White craft glue

1. Place the two pieces of paper together lengthwise so that they overlap by ½". Staple them together.

2. Roll the paper into a cone, making sure that the bottom is wide enough to fit your child's head. Overlap the paper at the seam and mark seam with a crayon.

3. Unroll the paper and cut off any excess.

4. Spread the paper flat and let your child use crayons and glitter to decorate one side of the paper.

5. Roll the paper back into a cone and staple it to create the hat.

Celebration Picture

Here is an unusual way for your child to create a festive picture.

ACTIVITY FOR AN INDIVIDUAL CHILD

Age group: 18–40 months

Duration of activity: 10 minutes

Tempera paint
Pie tins
Paper noisemakers
Construction paper or poster board
Confetti

1. Pour the paint into the pie tins.

2. Have your child dip the curled-up end of the noisemaker into the paint.

3. Show your child how to aim the noisemaker at the paper and have her blow. The goal is to have the painted tip of the noisemaker strike the paper and leave a mark.

4. While the paint is still wet, your child can sprinkle some confetti onto her picture.

Pot Banger

The classic stereotype is true: Toddlers love to bang on pots and pans. New Year's is the time to make a little noise anyhow, so why not have your child use a special pot-banging spoon?

ACTIVITY FOR AN INDIVIDUAL CHILD

Age group: 18–40 months

Duration of activity: 30 minutes

Tempera paint
Pie tins
Paintbrushes
Wooden kitchen spoon
White craft glue
Glitter
Ribbon (optional)

1. Pour the paint into the pie tins. Let your child paint the spoon however she wishes.

2. When the spoon is completely dry, show her how to coat the spoon with glue and then add glitter.

3. If you wish, tie a ribbon around the handle.

Valentine's Day

Love is in the air! Your toddler is just starting to learn about love and relationships. At this stage in his life, your toddler's greatest love is probably you. But soon, his social world will be expanding. Talk about love and caring while you do these projects with him. Here is a great chance to reinforce recognition of the colors pink and red, too.

Heart Prints

This activity will help your child develop fine motor skills. You may also want to use this as an opportunity to talk about color and shape identification. You don't have to limit your child to a simple sheet of paper. Perhaps she can print hearts onto a card or calendar.

ACTIVITY FOR AN INDIVIDUAL CHILD

Age group: 18–40 months

Duration of activity: 15 minutes

Red and pink tempera paint
Pie tins
Scissors
Kitchen sponges
Clothespins
White construction paper or bond paper

1. Pour the paint into the pie tins.

2. Cut out heart shapes from the sponges. You can make other shapes too. Be sure that the sponge shapes are at least as large as a silver dollar.

3. Attach a clothespin to the back of the sponge. This will serve as a handle for your child.

4. Show your child how to dip the sponge hearts into the paint and then press them onto the paper to create a design.

Kisses

This activity will be particularly enticing if you have a child who likes to put on mommy's makeup.

ACTIVITY FOR AN INDIVIDUAL CHILD

Age group: 30–40 months

Duration of activity: 10 minutes

Lipstick in a variety of colors
White construction or bond paper
Facial tissue

1. Help your child apply the lipstick.

2. Show your child how to kiss the paper to make lip prints. If you use more than one color of lipstick, help your child use the tissue to remove the preceding color.

Valentine's Card

Here is a cute idea for your child to create a truly personalized Valentine's Day card.

1. Fold the paper in half to create a card. On the front, write "Thumbody Loves You!"

2. Pour a small amount of the paint into the pie tin. Help your child to dip her thumb into the paint.

3. Open the card and show your child how to press her thumb onto the paper to create prints. Let her make as many thumbprints as she wishes to decorate the card.

St. Patrick's Day

It is said that anyone can be Irish on St. Patrick's Day. Focus on the color green and share some of the legends and lore of this holiday with your child.

Living Shamrock

This is a fun gardening activity, but it takes patience to see the result.

ACTIVITY FOR AN INDIVIDUAL CHILD

Age group: 18–40 months

Duration of activity: 15 minutes

Scissors
Kitchen sponge
Water
Shallow pie tin
Grass seeds

1. Cut the sponge into a shamrock shape.

2. Fill the pie tin with enough water to cover the bottom. Place the sponge in the water.

3. Help your child sprinkle the grass seeds onto the wet sponge.

4. Place the pie tin with the sponge in a sunny place. Keep the sponge moist while the grass is sprouting.

Rainbow's End

This cute craft makes a pretty centerpiece for a holiday party.
Add some gold-foil chocolate coins for extra excitement.

ACTIVITY FOR AN INDIVIDUAL CHILD

Age group: 30–40 months

Duration of activity: 15 minutes

Scissors
Toilet paper tube
Black felt-tip marker
Paper plate
Crayons or colored markers
White craft glue
Gold sequins

1. Cut the toilet paper tube in half crosswise. Discard one half.

2. Have your child color the half tube black to make the pot.

3. Cut the paper plate in half. Discard one half.

4. Cut off the rim of the plate to create an arch shape. You may need to trim the width so that one end will fit into the "pot."

5. Encourage your child to color the arch with rainbow colors.

6. Let your child glue some gold sequins to the rim of the little black pot.

7. Balance the rainbow arch by inserting one end of it into the pot opening.

Pot-of-Gold Hunt

You will be promoting your child's problem-solving skills while he plays this fun game. If you wish, you can substitute a real treat basket for the paper pot of gold; just be sure to decorate it with plenty of cut-out gold coins!

ACTIVITY FOR AN INDIVIDUAL CHILD

Age group: 30–40 months

Duration of activity: 20 minutes

Scissors
Colored construction paper
Masking tape

1. Cut the following shapes out of construction paper: 20 tiny green feet, 1 brown kettle, 10 small yellow circles, and an arch shape with different colors to form a rainbow.

2. Tape the yellow circles in the kettle shape to create the pot of gold.

3. Find a location to "hide" the pot of gold. Place it or tape it anywhere you wish.

4. Tape the green feet a few feet apart to form a path for your child to follow. Let them wind up the wall or under furniture to finally lead to the pot of gold.

5. Tell your child about how it is believed that a leprechaun can lead you to a pot of gold at the end of the rainbow. Show him the footprints, and encourage him to follow them to the treasure.

Passover and Purim

Both of these holidays occur in the spring and they both celebrate the Jewish people's freedom from oppression. These activities will help you introduce the history of Judaism and its culture to your toddler.

Matzo Ball Soup

This is a fun and tasty way to share a traditional holiday treat with your child.

ACTIVITY FOR AN INDIVIDUAL CHILD

Age group: 18–40 months
Duration of activity: 45 minutes

½ cup matzo meal
1 teaspoon salt
2 eggs, slightly beaten
2 tablespoons oil
8 cups plus 1 tablespoon water
8 chicken bouillon cubes
1 small can carrots

1. Mix the matzo meal with the salt.

2. Add the eggs and the oil. Help your child slowly stir in the tablespoon of water. The batter should be thick and pasty.

3. Chill the batter for 10–15 minutes. While the batter is chilling, boil the water and add the bouillon cubes. Once the cubes have dissolved, drain the can of carrots and add them to the soup.

4. Remove the matzo batter from the refrigerator. Show your child how to roll the mixture into golf ball-size balls. If the mixture is too sticky, try wetting your child's hands first.

5. Carefully drop the matzo balls into the boiling soup. Cover and simmer for 15–20 minutes.

Purim Gragger

Purim graggers are the noisemakers that children shake when the name of Haman is mentioned during the reading of the Meglliah. Be mindful that the loose beans could be a choking hazard; supervise the use of this toy carefully.

ACTIVITY FOR AN INDIVIDUAL CHILD

Age group: 18–40 months
Duration of activity: 15 minutes

White craft glue
Scraps of paper and ribbon
2 paper cups
¼ cup dried beans
Masking tape

1. Let your child glue paper and ribbon to the outside of the cups for decoration.

2. When the glue is dry, help her pour the beans into one of the cups.

3. Invert the second cup over the first and tape together.

Earth Day

It is not too early to start teaching your child to respect the earth and the environment. These simple activities are a great way to start.

Recycled Critters

There is no end to materials that you can use for this project.
Ask your friends and family to save things that you could use.

ACTIVITY FOR AN INDIVIDUAL CHILD

Age group: 30–40 months

Duration of activity: 20 minutes

A variety of recycled containers and objects such as: margarine tubs, toilet paper tubes, tissue boxes, lids, oatmeal canisters, buttons, soda bottles and fabric scraps

Glue or tape

Colored construction paper

Markers or crayons

1. Rinse out any containers, remove labels and check for sharp or loose parts.

2. Have your toddler glue or tape items together to create a creature.

3. Provide paper and markers or crayons for them to decorate.

4. Be sure to ask your toddler about what he made. Where does it live? What does it eat? Does it have a name?

Litter Grab

Older toddlers may enjoy joining in a community effort to pick up litter on earth day.

ACTIVITY FOR AN INDIVIDUAL CHILD

Age group: 18–40 months

Duration of activity: 15 minutes

Salad tongs or wire gripper
Plastic or paper bag

1. Select a site for your child to pick up litter. You may need to go in advance to remove glass, cigarette butts, or any other hazardous materials.

2. Show your child how to use the tongs to pick up litter and place into the bag.

Trash Sort

You will need to check for sharp edges and rinse out containers before starting this activity.

ACTIVITY FOR AN INDIVIDUAL CHILD

Age group: 24–40 months

Duration of activity: 15 minutes

Cleaned out plastic and glass containers and newspaper
Recycling bins

Demonstrate for your child how to sort the materials into glass, plastic and paper bins.

Easter

There are many symbols and traditions associated with this holiday. Easter eggs and the Easter Bunny may be the two most familiar to young children. Here are some simple activities that your toddler is sure to enjoy.

Footprint Bunny

Both you and your child will delight in this cute holiday craft. Don't worry if the end result does not look perfect—your child's creativity is more important than the finished result.

ACTIVITY FOR AN INDIVIDUAL CHILD

Age group: 30–40 months

Duration of activity: 15 minutes

White and pink construction paper
Pencil
Scissors
White craft glue
Cotton ball
6 (3") lengths of dark-colored yarn
Crayons

1. Have your child stand on a piece of white construction paper in stocking feet. Trace the outline of her foot.

2. Cut out the foot shape. Cut out two long ears from the pink paper.

3. Show your child how to make a bunny: glue the ears onto the heel end of the cut-out foot and the cotton ball to the toe end.

4. Let your child decorate her bunny with the yarn and crayons.

Easter Egg Dye

You do not have to rely on a store-bought kit to dye Easter eggs. Here are some creative ideas for you to try.

1. Make your own egg dye. In a coffee cup, combine ½ cup of boiling water, 1 teaspoon of vinegar, and ½ teaspoon of food coloring. Repeat this process for each color.

2. You can also make natural dyes. Natural dyes require the eggs to soak for much longer times, sometimes as long as overnight. Remember the longer the egg is in the dye, the darker the color will be. Some materials to try include onion skins, beet juice, and tea leaves.

Fourth of July

Your toddler is too young to understand the history behind this holiday. Keep it simple, and explain that you are celebrating the country's birthday. Your child will love being a part of the festivities.

Fireworks Painting

Your child will be practicing fine motor skills as he makes this colorful picture.
If you are worried that he will suck paint through the straw, take a pin and poke a
few small holes about ½" from the top of the straw.

ACTIVITY FOR AN INDIVIDUAL CHILD

Age group: 30–40 months

Duration of activity: 15 minutes

Spoon
Tempera paint, slightly thinned
White construction or bond paper
Straw

1. Let your child use the spoon to place small blobs of different colors of paint on the paper.

2. Show your child how to use the straw to blow the paint around on the paper, staying fairly close to the paper without allowing the straw to touch it. Let him experiment. What happens when he holds the straw straight up, and what happens when he tilts the straw?

Handmade Flag

Let your child express his patriotism with this personalized version of the American flag.
You can adapt this craft for any flag with stars.

ACTIVITY FOR AN INDIVIDUAL CHILD

Age group: 18–40 months

Duration of activity: 15 minutes

White craft glue
3 sheets white construction paper
1 sheet blue construction paper
Scissors
2 sheets red construction paper
White tempera paint
Shallow pie tin

1. Glue the white and blue papers side by side to form a large square, with the blue square in the top left corner.

2. Cut (or help your child cut) the red paper into ten strips. Glue six of the strips together end to end to create three long stripes. Glue the red stripes to the white part of the square, with the longer stripes at the bottom.

3. Pour some white paint into the pie tin. Help your child dip his hands in the paint, and then press his hands on the blue square to make stars. (Don't try for all fifty; instead, you're just going for the effect.)

Thanksgiving

The history of this holiday is more than your child can understand. Discussions about Pilgrims and Native Americans are not relevant to your child's experience of the world around her. The turkey, on the other hand, is a concrete symbol of the Thanksgiving meal. You may also choose to have a discussion about abundance and thankfulness during this holiday.

Turkey Trap

Engage your child's imagination with this activity. This may become a family tradition for years to come.

ACTIVITY FOR AN INDIVIDUAL CHILD

Age group: 18–40 months
Duration of activity: 15 minutes

1 cardboard box
1 sturdy stick
A few kernels of corn
Feathers
Candy corn

1. Tell your child that you are going to trap a turkey for Thanksgiving.

2. Set the cardboard box upside down and prop up one end with the stick. Show your child how the turkey will knock the stick over to make the box fall. Place some corn under the box to serve as bait.

3. Overnight, remove the corn and replace it with the feathers and candy corn. If you want, you can add a little note/poem from the Turkey: "You tried to catch me, but I can't be beat. So I left some candy for you to eat!"

Thanksgiving Tablecloth

Your toddler will feel that she is truly contributing to the holiday when she helps make this festive tablecloth.

ACTIVITY FOR AN INDIVIDUAL CHILD OR A GROUP

Age group: 18–40 months

Duration of activity: 20 minutes

1 large light-colored flat sheet (white or yellow works best)

Black fabric marker

Fabric paints

1. Spread the sheet somewhere with plenty of room for your child to work.

2. Have your child place her hand on the sheet palm down, with her fingers spread wide. Trace around her hand with the fabric marker. Repeat to create as many turkeys as she wishes. Perhaps the rest of the family will add their turkeys as well.

3. Allow her to use the fabric paint to embellish the turkeys and to add any other decoration that she wishes.

Chanukah

Chanukah is a Jewish holiday steeped in traditions. Don't forget to share some of your favorite ways to celebrate with your young child. This holiday lasts for eight days. Here are a few favorite activities to get you started with the celebration.

Handprint Menorah

This activity is a great way to reinforce Jewish holiday traditions as well as introduce your child to counting concepts.

ACTIVITY FOR AN INDIVIDUAL CHILD

Age group: 30–40 months

Duration of activity: 15 minutes

Blue tempera paint
Yellow tempera paint
2 pie tins
1 sheet construction paper

1. Pour the paint into separate pie tins. Have your child dip his hands in the blue paint and then press them flat onto the paper. His thumbs should overlap while his fingers should be spread apart.

2. Show him how the print resembles a menorah, with the thumb prints representing the Shamash. Count the eight candles with him.

3. Wash your child's hands. Then have him dip one finger into the yellow paint. Help him press his finger over each candle to make a flame.

Wooden Star of David

Your child will be learning about shapes and geometry while he makes this well-known symbol.

ACTIVITY FOR AN INDIVIDUAL CHILD

Age group: 18–40 months

Duration of activity: 20 minutes

6 craft sticks
White craft glue
Blue and white tempera paints
2 shallow pie tins
Paintbrushes

1. Show your child how to arrange three craft sticks to form a triangle. Have your child glue these sticks together. Repeat for a second triangle.

2. Once dry, show your child how to place one triangle upside down over the other triangle to create the Star of David. Glue the triangles in place.

3. Let the star dry. Pour paint into pie tins and let your child decorate the star.

I Am a Dreidel

Your toddler will enjoy spinning his body like a dreidel.
The song can be sung to the traditional dreidel tune or to "Row Row Row Your Boat."

ACTIVITY FOR AN INDIVIDUAL CHILD

Age group: 18–40 months
Duration of activity: 5 minutes

Teach your child the following song and then have him spin around while he sings it:

Dreidel, dreidel, dreidel,
I'm spinning all around.
Going slow and going fast
Until I'm on the ground.

Tube Menorah

With this menorah, you can add all of the flames at once or have your child
add a flame on each night of the holiday.

ACTIVITY FOR AN INDIVIDUAL CHILD

Age group: 30–40 months
Duration of activity: 20 minutes

Scissors
8 toilet paper tubes
1 paper towel tube
1 piece of cardboard 8" x 11"
White craft glue
Holiday gift wrap scraps
Yellow or orange tissue paper

1. Cut 4 (¼"-long) slits on one end of each tube. Fold these tabs back. Arrange the tubes on the cardboard—the tall tube in the center and four smaller tubes on each side. Glue in place.

2. Have your child glue the wrapping paper on the tubes for decoration. Encourage him to make the tall one (Shamash) stand out from the others.

3. Show your child how to crinkle a square of the tissue paper and stuff it into the top of a tube to represent a candle flame. Start with the center candle and do the same for all of the others.

Christmas

Even your young toddler will be aware of the hustle and bustle of the Christmas season. It is hard to shelter her from the music, the commercials, the movies, the decorations, and everything else. She does not have to be a passive bystander, though. These activities will encourage her to contribute festive decorations for your home.

Hanging Lids

This is a simple way to create attractive ornaments.
You may also use plastic lids, although it is harder to punch a hole in them.

ACTIVITY FOR AN INDIVIDUAL CHILD

Age group: 18–40 months
Duration of activity: 15 minutes

Hole punch
Lids from frozen juice cans
Pieces of yarn
Glitter, sequins, stickers, tinsel
White craft glue

1. Punch a hole ½" in from the edge of each lid. String and loop a piece of yarn so that your child can hang her ornament.

2. Have your child decorate both sides of the lids with the glitter and craft materials.

Handprint Wreath

This is a personalized holiday decoration. You may wish to do one with each member of your family.

ACTIVITY FOR AN INDIVIDUAL CHILD

Age group: 30–40 months

Duration of activity: 25 minutes

Scissors
Paper plate
Green and red construction paper
Pencil
White craft glue

1. Cut the flat center out of the paper plate so that only the rim remains.

2. Have your child spread her fingers and lay her hand flat on the green construction paper. Trace around your child's hand with the pencil to create a hand template.

3. Cut out a dozen hands from the template.

4. Cut out three red circles, about the size of a grape.

5. Help your child arrange the hands around the plate. You want the hands to overlap and the fingers to reach outward.

6. Help your child glue the hands to the plate. Let her glue on the red "berries" for a finishing touch.

Lacy Balls

You will be surprised at the elegant and delicate appearance of these ornaments.
Remember that balloon pieces can be a choking hazard for young children;
only an adult should pop the balloon and discard the pieces.

ACTIVITY FOR AN INDIVIDUAL CHILD

Age group: 18–40 months

Duration of activity: 1 hour

Plastic bowl
⅓ cup white craft glue
⅔ cup liquid laundry starch
Lengths of yarn 1"–7" long
Small inflated balloon

1. In the bowl, mix the white craft glue with the liquid laundry starch.

2. Show your toddler how to dip yarn into this mixture and drape around the blown-up balloon.

3. Have her repeat with additional yarn strands until a desired pattern or design is created. She should leave some gaps and not cover the balloon completely.

4. Once the yarn is dry, pop and remove the balloon.

Kwanzaa

Kwanzaa is a relatively new holiday. Take this opportunity to share with your young child the heritage and history of African Americans.

Kwanzaa Placemat (Mkeka)

This is a personalized holiday decoration. You may wish to do one with each member of your family.

ACTIVITY FOR AN INDIVIDUAL CHILD

Age group: 30–40 months

Duration of activity: 20 minutes

Black, green, and red construction paper
Scissors
Masking tape

1. Fold a piece of black construction paper in half crosswise.

2. Cut slits from the folded center to about 1" away from the edge. Space the slits 1" apart. Unfold the paper.

3. Cut out red and green strips just a little thinner than 1"and as long as the black paper.

4. Help your child weave the strips through the black paper. Alternate the red and green strips and be sure to push each one snug against the previous one. Don't worry if the pattern is not perfect.

5. Secure any loose ends with the tape.

Kwanzaa Colors

Here is a simple way to introduce your child to the traditional colors of Kwanzaa.

ACTIVITY FOR AN INDIVIDUAL CHILD

Age group: 18–30 months

Duration of activity: 15 minutes

White craft glue
Water
Paper cup
Paintbrush
Green and red tissue paper
Black construction paper

1. Mix the glue with a small amount of water in a paper cup. The glue should be thin enough to paint on the paper with a brush.

2. Let your toddler tear the tissue paper into shreds.

3. Have him lay out the tissue paper on the black construction paper.

4. Help him paint over the tissue paper with the glue solution. Be careful he does not saturate the paper so much that it is soaked through.

CHAPTER 18

Party Time

A birthday party can be a special and memorable occasion for your child. However, it can also become a time of stress, overexcitement, and chaos. The best way to plan for a successful children's party is to lower your expectations. Toddlers are easily impressed, so you don't need to hire the most popular performer around and a cast of thousands to entertain your guests. Your best bet is to keep things very simple. Invite only a few of your child's playmates, and keep the party short and uncomplicated. Refreshments, gift opening, and two or three simple activities is plenty.

Theme Parties

You don't need to have a fancy theme to have a successful birthday party for your child. But there are advantages to a theme party. It may be easier for you to decorate and plan for a party that revolves around a theme. You can adapt just about any menu or activity to fit your theme. For example, the game Pin the Tail on the Donkey can fit into any of the themes below if you simply change it to Pin the Ears on the Teddy Bear, Pin the Nose on the Clown, or Pin the Tiara on the Princess!

Teddy Bear's Picnic Theme Party

This is a great theme idea for an outdoor party.

ACTIVITY FOR A GROUP

Age group: 18–40 months
Duration of activity: 1 hour

1. Encourage children to bring their own teddy bears to join in the festivities. Be sure to have a few extra on hand for those who attend the party solo.

2. Weather permitting, serve refreshments outside on a picnic blanket. One themed menu idea is Teddy Grahams.

3. Put on some music and have guests dance with their teddy bears. They can also form a circle by holding hands with each other and the bears to play Ring Around the Rosy.

4. You can also create simple party hats for your guests. Create a headband from folded brown construction paper. Cut out brown bear ears for the children to glue on.

Princess Theme Party

Make your birthday girl feel special and make her princess for a day.

ACTIVITY FOR A GROUP

Age group: 18–40 months

Duration of activity: 1 hour

1. Let your guests get into character by making some props, such as crowns and magic wands. Be creative!

2. Be sure to have some old dresses and fancy accessories for the party guests to play dress up.

3. Before your guests sit down at the table for refreshments, have them decorate folding chairs to create their own thrones. Provide each child with an old pillow case. Cut off half of the length. Let the children decorate the pillow case with fabric paints. When they are dry, simply slip the covers on the backs of the chairs to create thrones.

Circus Theme Party

There are many fun ways to celebrate a circus theme. If you are considering inviting an entertainer for the party, keep in mind that many toddlers are fearful of clowns.

ACTIVITY FOR A GROUP

Age group: 18–40 months

Duration of activity: 1 hour

1. Let the children put on their own circus. Set out three hula hoops for the rings. Invite each child to take a turn stepping inside the ring to dance or perform.

2. Stretch a thick rope on the ground and challenge the guests to walk along it as if they were in a high-wire act.

3. No circus is complete without face painting. You will find a recipe in Appendix A.

Birthday Parties for Two-Year-Olds

Your child's second birthday will not hold much meaning for him. Recognize that children this age often have difficulty playing together. Have different options on hand that will let your young guests play on their own if they are not ready to join the group.

Follow the Path

You will need a fairly large space for this activity. Be sure that children are supervised so that they do not pick up the rope and tangle it around a playmate or themselves.

ACTIVITY FOR A GROUP

Age group: 18–40 months
Duration of activity: 15 minutes

1. Use a thick rope or cord to create a path for the children to follow. The more twists and turns you can make, the better. You can tape or weigh down sections of the rope to make them stay put.

2. Set up a surprise at the end of the path, such as a basket of party favors or the birthday cake.

Clap Your Hands

This is an easy music and movement activity to teach young children.
Use it when you sense your guests are getting restless.

ACTIVITY FOR A GROUP

Age group: 18–40 months
Duration of activity: 10 minutes

Teach the children the following song and movements:

> *Clap, clap, clap your hands,*
> *Clap your hands together.*
> *Clap, clap, clap your hands,*
> *Clap your hands together.*

Refrain: (hold one arm over your head and spin in a circle)

> *La la la la la la la*
> *La la la la la*
> *La la la la la la la*
> *La la la la la*

Other verses: *Stomp, stomp, stomp your feet; Shake, shake, shake your leg; Bend, bend, bend your knee; Nod, nod, nod your head.*

Birthday Blocks

Not all birthday games need to be group activities.
Two-year-olds often do best when simply playing side by side. Here is a fun play activity to have available.

ACTIVITY FOR AN INDIVIDUAL CHILD OR A GROUP

Age group: 18–40 months
Duration of activity: 15 minutes

Scissors
Tape
Gift wrap
Wooden building blocks
Clear contact paper

Use scissors and tape to wrap each building block like a miniature gift. Cover it in contact paper to keep the wrapping paper intact. Give the blocks to the children to build with.

Birthday Parties for Three-Year-Olds

For your child's third birthday, you can plan more involved activities. Children of this age have a longer attention span and are better able to follow directions.

Flour Bombs

This is strictly an outdoor activity and makes a fun alternative to water balloons. You may wish to set up a target or just let the children bomb the trees, pavement, and walls.

ACTIVITY FOR AN INDIVIDUAL CHILD

Age group: 30–40 months

Duration of activity: 15 minutes

Paper napkins
Flour
Masking tape

For each flour bomb, fill ½ of a paper napkin with flour. Bring up the ends of the napkin and twist. Secure the bomb with a little bit of masking tape.

Party Hats

Skip the store-bought party hats this year. Your guests will enjoy making their own.

ACTIVITY FOR AN INDIVIDUAL CHILD

Age group: 30–40 months

Duration of activity: 20 minutes

Construction paper
Stickers
Ribbons and bows
Confetti
White craft glue
Stapler

1. Let each child choose a sheet of colored construction paper. Have them decorate one side with stickers, ribbons, bows, and confetti.

2. When the paper is dry, you can fit the hat for each child. Roll each piece of paper into a cone so that the opening fits on the child's head. Staple the cone closed along the seam.

Group Craft Projects

A group craft project can be a fun way to involve all of the party guests, young and old alike. These activities focus more on the process than on the finished project.

Homemade Wrapping Paper

You can let the children take some of the paper home.
Alternatively, do this project at the beginning of the party and while the children are
preoccupied with something else, have someone use this paper to wrap the party favors.

ACTIVITY FOR A GROUP

Age group: 18–40 months

Duration of activity: 20 minutes

Scissors
Kitchen sponges
Butcher paper
Tempera paint
Pie tins
Wooden clothespins

1. Before the party cut the sponges into different shapes such as a party hat or birthday cake. If you are having a theme party, cut shapes that match the theme.

2. Seat your guests around a table covered with butcher paper.

3. Pour different colors of paint into the pie tins and show the children how to use the sponges as stamps. Attach the clothespins to the sponges if children are having difficulty grasping the sponges.

4. Encourage the children to create a design on all areas of the paper. Let dry before dividing or using.

Fence Tapestry

This is a great project if you have a cyclone fence in your yard. You will be surprised at how nice the
finished result looks. Be sure to take pictures of the completed results to send home. Supervise this
project carefully, and be mindful of any long materials that could pose a choking hazard.

ACTIVITY FOR A GROUP

Age group: 18–40 months

Duration of activity: 30 minutes

Various weaving materials, such as
    ribbons, foil scraps, newspaper strips,
    twigs, yarn, and old sheets or curtains

Show the children how to weave the different materials through the fence holes. The weaving technique does not have to be perfect or uniform. In fact, it will look better when children add materials in their own way.

Jumbo Card

Do this activity during a transition time in the party when children are arriving or leaving. Your child will be left with a special keepsake of the day.

ACTIVITY FOR A GROUP

Age group: 18–40 months

Duration of activity: 5 minutes

1 sheet poster board
Markers, crayons, and other decorating
 materials

1. Fold poster board in half and write "Happy Birthday" on the front. Attach a large bow on the top corner.

2. Set the card up in a location that is easy for the guests to reach. Supply them with crayons and markers for them to "sign" and decorate a message for the birthday child.

Giant Mural Puzzle

The nice thing about this activity is that the guests get to take puzzle pieces home with them. You may want to provide smocks, as this can be a messy activity.

ACTIVITY FOR A GROUP

Age group: 18–40 months

Duration of activity: 30 minutes

Butcher paper
Pie tins or pans
Tempera paints
Large paint brushes
Scissors

1. Hang a large sheet of butcher paper in a place where all the children can easily reach. Outdoors is best.

2. Give the children pans of tempera paint and large brushes. Encourage them to work together to paint a large mural.

3. You want children to work together, but you can also mark sections of the mural off with a pencil if necessary.

4. When the children are done, let the painting dry.

5. Cut the paper into equal sections. Give one to each child.

6. Distribute the sections and then challenge the children to put the mural puzzle back together again.

More Party Games

Here are more all-purpose party games. You will find that they are appropriate for a wide range of ages and abilities. They require few materials and little planning for those times when you need a little something extra to pass the time.

Pass the Beanbag

This fun game is similar to Hot Potato, but because it is noncompetitive, no one is eliminated.

ACTIVITY FOR A GROUP

Age group: 30–40 months

Duration of activity: 10 minutes

Beanbag or small ball

1. Have players sit cross-legged in a circle on the floor. Give the children the beanbag or ball and show them how to pass it around the circle.

2. While the children are passing the beanbag, teach them the song, sung to the tune of "Twinkle Twinkle Little Star":

   Pass the beanbag 'round the ring
   Pass the beanbag while we sing.
   Pass the beanbag to your friend
   In a circle without end.
   Pass the beanbag 'round the ring
   Pass the beanbag while we sing.

3. Once started, give directions on how to pass the beanbag (low, high, fast, or slow).

Sleeping Lions

As with many other activities in this chapter, you can adapt this game to meet the theme of your party.

ACTIVITY FOR A GROUP

Age group: 18–40 months
Duration of activity: 15 minutes

1. Divide the guests into two groups. One group is the lions; the other group is the safari photographers.

2. Instruct the lions to lie down and pretend to be sleeping.

3. The photographers are to sneak up as close as they can to take a picture without waking the lions.

4. When the lions awaken, they are to roar and scare away the other group.

5. Make sure that all children get a turn to be in both groups.

Blob Race

Although relay races may be too complex for young children, they will enjoy this simplified version.

ACTIVITY FOR A GROUP

Age group: 30–40 months
Duration of activity: 20 minutes

1. Divide the guests into two teams. Designate a starting and a finish line for the race.

2. On your signal, teams are to race to the finish line. The one rule is that all members must stay connected. You can have them run different heats with variations. They can form a train, hold hands, or make a giant hug circle. See what other ideas they can dream up.

Silly Says

Here is a simplified version of Simon Says. In this adaptation, the leader is not trying to "trick" anyone.

ACTIVITY FOR A GROUP

Age group: 18–40 months

Duration of activity: 20 minutes

1. Start the game with an adult as the leader to show the children how it is played. Then each child can take a turn being the leader.

2. The leader picks out a character to imitate and calls out the directions using that persona ("Barney says" or "the Easter Bunny says").

3. The leader tells the group what to do (jump, spin, or touch their noses).

Party Preparation and Props

As any party host knows, half the fun of having a party is in the anticipation and planning. Don't be afraid to involve your child and to let her make some small choices and decisions about her special day. Encourage her to participate in the preparation.

Napkin-Holder Place Cards

Here is a creative way to involve your toddler in the party preparations.

ACTIVITY FOR AN INDIVIDUAL CHILD

Age group: 18–40 months

Duration of activity: 20 minutes

Scissors
Wrapping paper or tissue paper
Toilet paper tubes
White craft glue
Stickers
Felt-tip marker
Address labels

1. For each napkin holder, cut a piece of wrapping paper or tissue paper to fit around the tube.

2. Help your toddler glue the paper onto the outside of the tube.

3. Let her attach decorative stickers on each tube.

4. Write the guest's name on the address label and affix it to the tube.

5. Roll and insert a colorful napkin.

Table Centerpiece

Your child will enjoy creating this festive and decorative centerpiece craft.

ACTIVITY FOR AN INDIVIDUAL CHILD

Age group: 18–40 months

Duration of activity: 30 minutes

2 sheets construction paper
Empty coffee can
White craft glue
Scissors
Colored tissue paper
Shallow pie tin

1. Help your child roll the construction paper sheets to cover the outside of the coffee can. Let her glue the paper on.

2. Trim off any extra paper.

3. Let your child rip the tissue paper into tiny squares.

4. Show your child how to crumple up each square to create a tiny ball or blossom.

5. Pour a small amount of glue into the pie tin. Have your child dip each tissue wad into the glue and stick it onto the can.

6. When your child is done decorating the can in this fashion, let it dry.

7. Use the container to hold flowers or balloons.

Party Photo Frames

What better party favor than a reminder of all the fun times!

ACTIVITY FOR A GROUP

Age group: 18–40 months

Duration of activity: 30 minutes

Scissors
Poster board
Felt-tip marker
Confetti
Glitter
White craft glue
Instant or digital camera

1. For each frame, cut a square of poster board 2" larger than the diameter of the picture you will be using.

2. Cut out a square from the center of the poster board, leaving a 1½" frame.

3. Use the marker to write a title on the top of the frame, such as "Tony's 2nd Birthday Party."

4. Let each child decorate her own frame with the confetti and glitter.

5. Take the pictures while the frames are drying. If you cannot make reproductions of one picture, go ahead and snap similar poses for each picture—they don't have to be identical. Pose the children in a group. Don't push for perfect smiles. Let them be a little silly and capture the true fun they are having.

6. Attach a photo behind each frame with a small dab of glue or rubber cement.

Recipes for Activity Materials

Paint

Puffy Paint

This is a great way for your child to add some texture to her art work.

Makes 1½ cups

Age group: 18–40 months

Duration of activity: 10 minutes

1 cup flour

½ cup salt

¼ cup water

4 tablespoons poster or tempera paint

Mix all of the ingredients together.

Flour Finger Paint

Save some money. For another cost-cutting idea, you can use freezer wrap instead of expensive finger-paint paper.

Makes 3 cups

Age group: 18–40 months

Duration of activity: 10 minutes

3 cups flour

2 tablespoons liquid soap

¾ cup water

Food coloring

Mix all the ingredients together. Use a spoon to put a blob of it on the paper for your child.

Face Paint

Easy to apply, easy to wash off. Now your child can be a clown for the day!

Variable Yield

Age group: 18–40 months

Duration of activity: 10 minutes

1 part cornstarch

½ part water

½ part cold cream

Food coloring

Mix all the ingredients together and apply with cotton swabs.

Salt Paint

Add a new dimension to your child's painting. When this paint dries, it sparkles.

Makes ½ cup

Age group: 18–40 months

Duration of activity: 10 minutes

¼ cup liquid starch

¼ cup water

2 tablespoons tempera paint

Mix all the ingredients together.

Finger Paint

In addition to a great sensory experience, finger painting helps your child develop fine motor skills.

Makes ½ cup

Age group: 18–40 months

Duration of activity: 10 minutes

2 cups cold water

3 teaspoons sugar

½ cup cornstarch

Food coloring

Add the water to the first two ingredients and cook over a low heat.

Stir constantly until the mixture is blended together.

Remover from the heat and add food coloring as desired.

Shiny Paint

With ingredients that you could have in your kitchen pantry, you can create an interesting paint that is shiny when it dries.

Variable Yield

Age group: 18–40 months

Duration of activity: 10 minutes

Food coloring

Light corn syrup or condensed milk

Simply add a few drops of food coloring to light corn syrup or condensed milk. The paint will be sticky but will dry with a nice glossy effect.

Easy Paint

Try this recipe when you run out of tempera paint or you just want to try something different.

Variable Yield

Age group: 18–40 months

Duration of activity: 10 minutes

1 part vinegar

1 part cornstarch

Food coloring

Put all ingredients into a jar. Close the lid and shake until the ingredients are well mixed.

Thick Paint

Try this paint for a variation with texture.

Makes 1½ cups

Age group: 18–40 months

Duration of activity: 10 minutes

1 cup powdered tempera paint

2 tablespoons wallpaper paste

½ cup liquid laundry starch

Mix the paint and paste together. Add in the starch gradually until you reach desired consistency.

Watercolor Paints

You can use bottle caps or empty egg cartons for paint tins.

Variable Yield

Age group: 18–40 months

Duration of activity: 10 minutes

1 tablespoon white vinegar

2 tablespoons baking powder

1 tablespoon corn flour

½ teaspoon glycerin

2 drops food coloring

1 teaspoon water

Mix the vinegar and baking soda together. Stir until it stops fizzing.

Add the remaining ingredients. Pour into molds and let harden.

Faux Oil Paint

Here is an easy paint recipe to try.

Variable Yield

Age group: 18–40 months

Duration of activity: 10 minutes

1 part liquid dish soap

1 part powdered tempera paint

Mix the ingredients together.

Stiff Paint

You can use this for regular or finger painting.

Variable Yield

Age group: 18–40 months

Duration of activity: 10 minutes

1 part nonmenthol shaving cream

1 part white craft glue

Food coloring

Mix ingredients together.

Dough

Cold Playdough

So easy you can let your child help make it!

Makes 2 cups

Age group: 18–40 months

Duration of activity: 10 minutes

1 cup salt

1 cup flour

½ cup water

Food coloring

Mix all ingredients together to proper consistency. Add in a few drops of food coloring. Store in airtight containers.

Cooked Playdough

This recipe produces a wonderful modeling dough that does not harden.

Makes 1½ cups

Age group: 18–40 months

Duration of activity: 10 minutes

½ cup salt

1 cup flour

1 cup water

1 tablespoon cooking oil

1 tablespoon cream of tartar

Food coloring

Mix all ingredients together and cook in a saucepan over a low heat.

Remove from the heat when the mixture starts to clump to resemble mashed potatoes.

While the mixture is cooling, knead in a few drops of food coloring. Store in airtight containers.

Cooked Playdough 2

Try this variation to make a soft and pliable dough.

Makes 1½ cups

Age group: 18–40 months

Duration of activity: 20 minutes

1 cup flour

1 tablespoon alum

½ cup salt

1 tablespoon oil

1 cup water

2 tablespoons vanilla

Food coloring

Stir together dry ingredients, then add the oil and water.

Cook over low heat, stirring constantly.

When the mixture reaches the consistency of mashed potatoes, remove from heat.

Let cool, then knead in the vanilla and the food coloring.

Peppermint Playdough

Your child will love the unique scent. You can also experiment with other extracts.

Makes 3½ cups

Age group: 18–40 months

Duration of activity: 10 minutes

2 cups warm water

2 cups flour

1 cup salt

4 teaspoons cream of tartar

4 tablespoons oil

4 tablespoons peppermint extract

Red food coloring

Mix the first six ingredients together. Stir until the dough pulls away from the side of the bowl.

Divide the dough into two balls and knead the red coloring into one ball.

Show your child how to twist and blend the two colors together.

Peanut Butter Playdough

You know that your child is going to put it in her mouth anyway! Please note that honey is not safe for children under the age of one.

Variable Yield

Age group: 18–40 months

Duration of activity: 10 minutes

1 part peanut butter

1 part nonfat powdered milk

1 teaspoon honey (optional)

Mix all ingredients together.

Cloud Dough

This dough has a springy texture.

Variable Yield

Age group: 18–40 months

Duration of activity: 10 minutes

1 part salad oil

6 parts flour

1 part water

Mix the oil and flour together.

Gradually add water until the desired consistency is reached.

Oatmeal Fundough

This dough has a unique texture. It is edible but does not taste good. In addition, it does not store well, so go ahead and throw it away after your child is done playing.

Makes 2 cups

Age group: 18–40 months

Duration of activity: 10 minutes

2 cups uncooked oatmeal

1 cup flour

¼ cup water

Mix all the ingredients together. Let your child knead the dough.

Rubber Dough

You will be surprised at the unique texture of this dough.

Makes 2 cups

Age group: 18–40 months

Duration of activity: 15 minutes

2 cups baking soda

1½ cups water

1 cup cornstarch

Combine all ingredients in a saucepan over a medium heat. Stir until mixture reaches a boil.

When the dough is thick, remove it from the heat and cool it on a flat surface.

Store in airtight containers.

Kool-Aid Dough

A very popular dough, this looks and smells terrific.

Makes 2 cups

Age group: 18–40 months

Duration of activity: 10 minutes

1 cup sifted flour

½ cup salt

3 tablespoons oil

1 package Kool-Aid

1 cup boiling water

Mix all the ingredients together. Once the mixture cools, let your child knead the dough.

Pumpkin Pie Dough

Here is fun seasonal dough. Be warned that it does not taste as good as it smells!

Makes 2 cups

Age group: 18–40 months

Duration of activity: 20 minutes

5½ cups flour

2 cups salt

8 teaspoons cream of tartar

¾ cup oil

1 ounce pumpkin-pie spice

Orange food coloring

4 cups water

Mix all the ingredients together over low heat.

Stir constantly until mixture reaches the consistency of mashed potatoes.

Remove from heat. When cool, knead.

Mud Dough

Your child will love this dough's muddy texture.

Makes 2½ cups

Age group: 18–40 months

Duration of activity: 10 minutes

½ cup cold water

1 tablespoon oil

2 tablespoons brown tempera paint

½ cup salt

1 tablespoon cornstarch

1½ cups flour

Mix the water, oil, and paint together.

Stir in the remaining ingredients and knead together.

Snow Dough

This dough has a very nice appearance and texture.

Variable Yield

Age group: 18–40 months

Duration of activity: 10 minutes

2 parts flour

1 part salt

Water

White tempera paint powder

White glitter

Mix all the flour and salt together.

Gradually add water until you reach the desired consistency.

Sprinkle in the white tempera powder and glitter for color and effect.

Bread Dough

This dough is great for fine detailed work. When it dries, it looks like porcelain.

Variable Yield

Age group: 18–40 months

Duration of activity: 10 minutes

White bread without crust

White craft glue

Food coloring

Let your child shred bread into tiny pieces.

Add glue and have your child knead the dough until it reaches a proper consistency (not too gooey).

Add either bread or glue as needed. Add a few drops of coloring as desired.

Clay

Homemade Clay

The thicker the sculpture, the longer it takes to dry.

Makes 3 cups

Age group: 18–40 months

Duration of activity: 30 minutes

2 cups baking soda

1 cup cornstarch

1¼ cups cold water

Mix all the ingredients together and cook over a medium heat while stirring constantly.

When mixture reaches the consistency of mashed potatoes, remove from the heat and place on a clean counter or plate.

Cover the clay with a damp cloth until it is cool.

Knead the clay, and mold and sculpt as desired.

Toothpaste Clay

This is an unusual clay. Your child can squish and mold it like putty, but it will dry overnight.

Variable Yield

Age group: 18–40 months

Duration of activity: 10 minutes

1 part toothpaste (not gel)
2 parts white glue
4 parts cornstarch
1 part water
1–2 drops food coloring

Mix toothpaste, glue, and cornstarch together. Gradually add water and food coloring.

Dryer Lint Clay

You will be amazed at the result of this project.

Makes 3½ cups

Age group: 18–40 months

Duration of activity: 20 minutes

3 cups dryer lint
2 cups cold or warm water
⅔ cup flour
3 drops oil of cloves

Mix the first three ingredients in a saucepan over low heat. Stir constantly to prevent lumps.

Add the oil of cloves. Continue stirring until peaks form.

Remove from heat and let cool. You can shape this by hand or place in molds.

Dry for three or four days.

Holiday Ornaments

This clay hardens in the oven.

Makes 3 cups

Age group: 18–40 months

Duration of activity: 45 minutes

1½ cups flour
1½ cups cinnamon and nutmeg mix
1 cup salt
1 cup water
Holiday cookie cutters
1 straw

Mix all the ingredients together. Add more water if dough is dry and does not hold together.

Have your child knead the dough and then roll it out to a disc ¼" thick.

Show your child how to cut out shapes from the dough using cookie cutters.

Use the straw to poke a small hole in the top of the ornament.

Bake at 300°F for ½ hour or until the ornaments are hard.

Chalk

Spray Chalk

Your child can spray this on beach sand or snow.

Makes ½ cup

Age group: 18–40 months

Duration of activity: 10 minutes

1 cup water
4 tablespoons cornstarch
3 drops food coloring

Mix all the ingredients and put into spray bottles.

Eggshell Chalk

This chalk is only for sidewalk use.

Makes 1 stick

Age group: 18–40 months

Duration of activity: 20 minutes

4 eggshells
1 teaspoon flour
1 teaspoon very hot tap water

Grind clean dry eggshells to a fine powder.

Add 1 tablespoon of this power to the flour and hot water.

Mix until a paste forms.

Roll paste into a cylinder and wrap in waxed paper.

Allow to dry for three days, then remove the paper.

Sidewalk Chalk

Homemade chalk is cheaper, and creates less dust.

Variable Yield

Age group: 18–40 months

Duration of activity: 3 hours

2 cups water
2 cups plaster of Paris
2 tablespoons powdered tempera paint

Stir all ingredients in a large bowl and let set for a few minutes.

Spoon the mixture into molds. (Tape one end of a toilet paper tube closed to create a jumbo chalk mold.)

Let chalk dry for at least three hours before removing from the mold.

Miscellaneous Materials

Silly Putty

This project is messy, but the result is nicer than the commercial product. Sometimes this is also called slime or ooze.

Variable Yield

Age group: 18–40 months

Duration of activity: 15 minutes

2 parts white craft glue or starch
1 part liquid starch

Mix together. If the mixture stays stringy, add a drop of glue. If it's too brittle, add more starch.

Chill for at least three hours.

Add either glue or starch as needed. Add a few drops of coloring as desired.

Goop

This is a messy but fun sensory material.

Variable Yield

Age group: 18–40 months

Duration of activity: 10 minutes

2 parts cornstarch
1 part water

Let your child use his hands to mix the ingredients together in a shallow bowl or container.

Have him explore what happens when he adds more water or cornstarch.

Jewels and Gems

Mix this up in a large dish bin.

Variable Yield

Age group: 18–40 months

Duration of activity: 3 hours

2 cups rock salt

6 to 8 drops food coloring

½ cup white craft glue

Waxed paper

Mix the salt and food coloring together.

Add the glue and mix thoroughly.

Mold into gem and jewel shapes.

Set on waxed paper to dry.

Super Bubbles

Here is a bubble solution that will form more durable bubbles than the solution you buy at the store.

Makes 1½ cups

Age group: 18–40 months

Duration of activity: 10 minutes

1 cup water

2 tablespoons light corn syrup

4 tablespoons liquid dish soap

Mix all ingredients in a jar or container with a secure lid.

Lick-and-Stick Stickers

Now your child can make his own stickers, and they will taste good too!

Makes ½ cup

Age group: 18–40 months

Duration of activity: 30 minutes

2 tablespoons boiling water

1 tablespoon flavored gelatin

Shallow cup or dish

Decorated bond paper or magazine and newspaper clippings

Cotton swabs

Add the boiling water to the gelatin powder; stir until dissolved.

When it is cool, place the mixture in a shallow cup or dish and your child can use it as sticker glue. Stickers can be made of bond paper or even magazine and newspaper clippings. Show him how to use the swabs to paint on the glue.

When the glue is dry, your child can lick and stick the sticker wherever he wants.

Classroom Paste

It is not hard to make a paste similar to the one you remember from elementary school.

Makes 1½ quarts

Age group: 18–40 months

Duration of activity: 10 minutes

1 cup flour

1 cup sugar

1 cup cold water

4 cups boiling water

1 tablespoon alum

½ teaspoon oil of wintergreen

Mix flour and sugar in bowl, then slowly add in cold water to make a paste.

Add the boiling water and transfer the mixture to a saucepan.

Bring to a boil and stir until mixture is thick and clear.

Remove from the heat and add the alum and oil of wintergreen.

Recommended Resources

Other Toddler Activity Books

Herr, Judy. *Creative Learning Activities for Young Children.* (New York: Delmar Thomson Learning, 2000).

Kohl, MaryAnn. *First Art: Art Experiences for Toddlers and Twos.* (Silver Spring, Maryland: Gryphon House, 2002).

Masi, Wendy. *Toddler Play (Gymboree).* (Minneapolis, MN: Creative Publishing International, 2001).

Pica, Rae. *Moving and Learning Series: Toddlers.* (New York: Delmar Thomson Learning, 2000).

Rowley, Barbara. *Baby Days: Activities, Ideas, and Games for Enjoying Daily Life with a Child Under Three.* (New York, NY: Hyperion, 2000).

Schiller, Pam. *The Complete Resource Book for Toddlers and Twos: Over 2000 Experiences and Ideas.* (Silver Spring, Maryland: Gryphon House, 2003).

Warren, Jean. *Toddler Games: Simple Seasonal Games Designed Especially for Toddlers.* (Totline Publications, 2002)

Parenting Books

Bowers, Ellen. *The Everything® Toddler Book, 2nd Edition.* (Avon, MA: Adams Media, 2010).

Brazelton, T. Berry. *Touchpoints.* (Boston, MA: Da Capo Press, 1992).

Douglas, Ann. *The Mother of All Toddler Books.* (New York, NY: John Wiley & Sons, 2004).

Eisenberg, Arlene. *What to Expect: The Toddler Years.* (New York, NY: Workman Publishing Company, 1994).

Hewitt, Deborah. *So This Is Normal Too?* (St. Paul, MN: Redleaf Press, 1995).

Margulis, Jennifer, ed. *Toddler: Real-Life Stories of Those Fickle, Irrational, Urgent, Tiny People We Love.* (Jackson, TN: Seal Press, 2003).

Murphy, Jana. *The Secret Lives of Toddlers: A Parent's Guide to the Wonderful, Terrible, Fascinating Behavior of Children Ages 1–3.* (New York, NY: Perigee Trade, 2004).

Shonkoff, Jack P., ed. *From Neurons to Neighborhoods: The Science of Early Childhood Development.* (Washington, DC: National Academies Press, 2000).

Books for Your Toddler

Breeze, L., and A. Morris. *This Little Baby's Bedtime.* (New York, NY: Little, Brown and Company, 1990).

Brown, Margaret Wise. *Goodnight Moon.* (New York, NY: Harper Festival; board edition, 1991).

Carle, Eric. *The Very Hungry Caterpillar.* (New York, NY: Philomel, 1994).

Christelow, Eileen. *Five Little Monkeys Jumping on the Bed.* (New York, NY: Clarion Books, 1998).

Eastman, P. D., illus. *Are You My Mother?* (New York, NY: Random House Books for Young Readers; board edition, 1998).

Keats, Ezra Jack. *The Snowy Day.* (New York, NY: Viking Books; board edition, 1996).

Kingsley, Emily Perl. *I Can Do It Myself.* (Racine, WI: Western Publishing Co., Inc., 1980).

Kunhardt, Dorothy. *Pat the Bunny.* (New York, NY: Golden Books; reissue edition, 2001).

Westcott, Nadine Bernard. *I Know an Old Lady Who Swallowed a Fly.* (New York, NY: Little, Brown and Company, 1988).

Index

We Have

EVERYTHING®

on Anything!

The Everything® list spans a wide range of subjects, with more than 500 titles covering 25 different categories:

Business	History	Reference
Careers	Home Improvement	Religion
Children's Storybooks	Everything Kids	Self-Help
Computers	Languages	Sports & Fitness
Cooking	Music	Travel
Crafts and Hobbies	New Age	Wedding
Education/Schools	Parenting	Writing
Games and Puzzles	Personal Finance	
Health	Pets	